Contents

KU-163-654

The author and series editors

Guy Cook is Professor of Applied Linguistics at the University of Reading. He has worked as a schoolteacher in Egypt, Italy, and the UK, and as a lecturer at the University of Moscow and at the University of Leeds, and as head of languages at the London University Institute of Education. His publications include *The Discourse of Advertising* (1992) and *Discourse and Literature* (1994). He is co-editor (with Barbara Seidlhofer) of *Principle and Practice in Applied Linguistics* (1995). A new book on the role of language play in language learning will appear shortly.

Christopher N. Candlin is Chair Professor of Applied Linguistics and Director of the Centre for English Language Education and Communication Research at the City University of Hong Kong. His previous post was as Professor of Linguistics in the School of English, Linguistics, and Media, and Executive Director of the National Centre for English Language Teaching and Research at Macquarie University, Sydney, having earlier been Professor of Applied Linguistics and Director of the Centre for Language in Social Life at the University of Lancaster. He also co-founded and directed the Institute for English Language Education at Lancaster, where he focused on issues in in-service education for teachers and teacher professional development.

Henry Widdowson, previously Professor of English for Speakers of Other Languages at the University of London Institute of Education and Professor of Applied Linguistics at the University of Essex, is Professor of English Linguistics at the University of Vienna. He was previously Lecturer in Applied Linguistics at the University of Edinburgh. Before that, he worked on materials development and teacher education as a British Council English Language Officer in Sri Lanka and Bangladesh.

Through work with The British Council, The Council of Europe, and other agencies, both Editors have had extensive and varied experience of language teaching, teacher education, and curriculum development overseas, and both contribute to seminars, conferences, and professional journals.

Introduction

Discourse

Discourse analysis examines how stretches of language, considered in their full textual, social, and psychological context, become meaningful and unified for their users. It is a rapidly expanding field, providing insights into the problems and processes of language use and language learning, and is therefore of great importance to language teachers. Traditionally, language teaching has concentrated on pronunciation, grammar, and vocabulary, and while these remain the basis of foreign language knowledge, discourse analysis can draw attention to the skills needed to put this knowledge into action and to achieve successful communication.

This book aims to explain the theory of discourse analysis and to demonstrate its practical relevance to language learning and teaching. Section One examines the most important theoretical approaches. Section Two explores ways in which the knowledge described in Section One can be put into action for language learners, and the extent to which existing exercises and activities develop discourse skills. Section Three, through a series of tasks, suggests how practising teachers can try out, critically, the ideas of the other two sections, thus hopefully reaching their own conclusions, and making their own contribution to both theory and practice. The foreign language classroom provides discourse analysis with one of its best sources of observation and its most rigorous testing grounds for theory.

A book on discourse demands data. I have tried to choose my examples from a wide range of discourse types. Where sources are not given, the data are from my own transcriptions of the discourse of my family, students, friends and acquaintances, and where it is invented, this is clearly indicated in the text.

One stylistic point needs comment. There is now no choice among the pronouns referring to general cases which does not attract attention, and either the support or antagonism of the reader. 'He/she' and 's/he' seem clumsy, but as I wanted to avoid 'he', I have opted for the rather long-winded 'he or she' in some instances, and just 'she' or 'they' in others. I do not imply that linguistic change is all that is needed—but fewer 'he's are probably for the best.

There are several people I want to thank for their friendship and help.

The hard work and foresight of the two series editors has made the Scheme possible, and they have given me a great deal of detailed and constructive advice. In particular, my thanks go to Henry Widdowson, who gave me the opportunity, the inspiration, and the confidence to write this book. Anne Conybeare and Jennifer Bassett edited—and improved—my manuscript with meticulous attention to detail. My colleague Tony Cowie provided constant encouragement, and fertile discussion of many relevant issues. Julie Ashworth and John Clark, by sharing the development of their work, made me think harder about my own. Lastly, my thanks to Elena Poptsova-Cook, not for being the docile domestic protectress of the traditional male preface, but for discussing, contesting, and adding to these ideas.

Guy Cook

Language Teaching:
A Scheme for Teacher Education

The purpose of this scheme of books is to engage language teachers in a process of continual professional development. We have designed it so as to guide teachers towards the critical appraisal of ideas and the informed application of these ideas in their own classrooms. The scheme provides the means for teachers to take the initiative themselves in pedagogic planning. The emphasis is on critical enquiry as a basis for effective action.

We believe that advances in language teaching stem from the independent efforts of teachers in their own classrooms. This independence is not brought about by imposing fixed ideas and promoting fashionable formulas. It can only occur where teachers, individually or collectively, explore principles and experiment with techniques. Our purpose is to offer guidance on how this might be achieved.

The scheme consists of three sub-series of books covering areas of enquiry and practice of immediate relevance to language teaching and learning. Sub-series 1 (of which this present volume forms a part) focuses on areas of *language knowledge*, with books linked to the conventional levels of linguistic description: pronunciation, vocabulary, grammar, and discourse. Sub-series 2 focuses on different *modes of behaviour* which realize this knowledge. It is concerned with the pedagogic skills of speaking, listening, reading, and writing. Sub-series 3 focuses on a variety of *modes of action* which are needed if this knowledge and behaviour is to be acquired in the operation of language teaching. The books in this sub-series have to do with such topics as syllabus design, the content of language course, and aspects of methodology and evaluation.

This sub-division of the field is not meant to suggest that different topics can be dealt with in isolation. On the contrary, the concept of a scheme implies making coherent links between all these different areas of enquiry and activity. We wish to emphasize how their integration formalizes the complex factors present in any teaching process. Each book, then, highlights a particular topic, but also deals contingently with other issues, themselves treated as focal in other books in the series. Clearly, an enquiry into a mode of behaviour like speaking, for example, must also refer to aspects of language knowledge which it realizes. It must also connect to modes of action which can be directed at developing this behaviour in learners. As elements of the whole scheme, therefore, books cross-refer both within and across the different sub-series.

This principle of cross-reference which links the elements of the scheme is also applied to the internal design of the different inter-related books within it. Thus, each book contains three sections, which, by a combination of text and task, engage the reader in a principled enquiry into ideas and practices. The first section of each book makes explicit those theoretical ideas which bear on the topic in question. It provides a conceptual framework for those sections which follow. Here the text has a mainly *explanatory* function, and the tasks serve to clarify and consolidate the points raised. The second section shifts the focus of attention to how the ideas from Section One relate to activities in the classroom. Here the text is concerned with *demonstration*, and the tasks are designed to get readers to evaluate suggestions for teaching in reference both to the ideas from Section One and also to their own teaching experience. In the third section this experience is projected into future work. Here the set of tasks, modelled on those in Section Two, are designed to be carried out by the reader as a combination of teaching techniques and action research in the actual classroom. It is this section that renews the reader's contact with reality: the ideas expounded in Section One and linked to pedagogic practice in Section Two are now to be systematically *tested out* in the process of classroom teaching.

If language teaching is to be a genuinely professional enterprise, it requires continual experimentation and evaluation on the part of practitioners whereby in seeking to be more effective in their pedagogy they provide at the same time—and as a corollary—for their own continuing education. It is our aim in this scheme to promote this dual purpose.

Christopher N. Candlin
Henry Widdowson

Explanation
Theories of discourse

1 What is discourse?

1.1 Introduction

Much language study, and a good deal of language teaching, has always been devoted to sentences. Yet we all know, even if we submit to this approach as a temporary—and perhaps very fruitful—measure, that there is more to using language, and communicating successfully with other people, than being able to produce correct sentences. Not all sentences are interesting, relevant, or suitable; one cannot just put any sentence after another and hope that it will mean something. People do not always speak—or write—in complete sentences, yet they still succeed in communicating. Knowing what is supposed to make a sentence correct, and where that sentence ends, though it may be important and worth teaching and learning, is clearly not enough.

Nor is this only a question of a difference between writing and speech, as might at first appear.

▶ TASK 1

Here are two pieces of language:

A This box contains, on average, 100 Large Plain Paper Clips. 'Applied Linguistics' is therefore not the same as 'Linguistics'. The tea's as hot as it could be. This is Willie Worm. Just send 12 Guinness 'cool token' bottle tops.

B Playback. Raymond Chandler. Penguin Books in association with Hamish Hamilton. To Jean and Helga, without whom this book could never have been written. One. The voice on the telephone seemed to be sharp and peremptory, but I didn't hear too well what it said—partly because I was only half awake and partly because I was holding the receiver upside down.

1 Which of these two stretches of language is part of a unified whole?
2 What sort of text is it?
3 What is the other one?
4 How did you distinguish between them?

The first three questions are not difficult to answer, but they do illustrate a point. The fourth is more complex. The first piece, which happens to consist of five correct sentences, one spoken to me, and the rest written on objects and on pages around me, simply does not make sense. It gives no feeling of unity. The second, which has only one complete sentence out of six units bounded by full stops, very clearly *does* make sense (at least it seems fair to predict that for most people it will). It also seems reasonable to assume that you, the reader, apart from making sense of it, could, if asked, give a large amount of information about it which is not explicitly expressed in it. You could restore the original layout and typography, identify the genre, the title, the publisher, the author, the dedication, make a guess at the identity of Jean and Helga, say that this is only the beginning of something, predict possible continuations, say whether you would read on . . . and answer many other questions besides.

The quality of being meaningful and unified, which the second passage has but the first passage lacks, is known as *coherence*. It is a quality which is clearly necessary for communication and therefore for foreign language learning, but which cannot be explained by concentrating on the internal grammar of sentences.

So we are left with two problems. Firstly, why have teachers and students of language concentrated so exclusively upon the production of correct sentences if that is not enough to communicate? Secondly, if it is not the rules of the sentence that enable us to be meaningful and to perceive meaning, then what is it? Let us look at the first problem first.

1.2 Sentence study in language teaching and linguistics

In defence of concentrating on the sentence, different teachers and different learners might give different answers. Teachers of mother tongue students might argue that their students already have oral and communicative skills, that what they need is to learn and demonstrate literacy, that putting full stops in the right place and writing grammatical sentences is a sign of this literacy. They might also point out that these skills, rightly or wrongly, are demanded by examination boards, and are often considered a sign of acceptable language behaviour by the world at large. Foreign language teachers might say that their students already know how to communicate and interact in their own language; what they need in the foreign language are formal skills and knowledge—pronunciation, vocabulary, grammar— which will provide the basis for communicating and interacting. Exercises, whether for translation or other kinds of manipulation, can be neatly presented in sentences, with a tick or a mark for each one, and in this way everybody knows where they are going, and how far they have come in developing the necessary formal basis. Given practice and exposure, it is argued, and maybe a trip to the country where the language is spoken, the rest will follow of its own accord.

We all know, and laugh at, the ludicrous examples which this concentration on the sentence can lead to in language teaching books: examples which seem very remote from our usual experience of communication. Nearly a hundred years ago, the phonetician Henry Sweet (the model for Shaw's Professor Higgins in *Pygmalion*) parodied the kind of monstrosity produced for translation exercises:

> 'The philosopher pulled the lower jaw of the hen.'
> 'The merchant is swimming with the gardener's son, but the Dutchman has the fine gun.'
> (*Sweet 1899 [1964:73]*)

Good tests of vocabulary and grammar maybe; but when would we ever use them? Yet though we laugh at them, we seem still to believe in their usefulness. The sentence 'He has some deaf black slave girls' (Tritton 1943:72), for example, is not another of Sweet's humorous inventions but a sentence for translation from the edition of *Teach Yourself Arabic*, in print until 1984: one of the best-selling series of foreign language textbooks in Britain.

Another argument for concentrating on artificially constructed sentences has sometimes been advanced by people involved in *linguistics* (the study of how human language in general works, rather than of how to speak a particular one). It is sometimes argued that even if the sentences analysed in linguistics are abstractions, which sometimes sound very odd, they are still the best material for language study, because they isolate it from its context. Furthermore, it is said, as native speakers of a language seem able to recognize correct and incorrect sentences, the idea of there being language rules exemplified in such sentences does seem to correspond to some kind of reality, even if people do not always speak according to these abstracted rules. Some might go further and add that, contrary to popular—and some scholarly—belief, people do, in any case, usually speak in well-formed sentences. Halliday (1985b:35), for example, claims that 'impeccably well formed [language] is typical of casual spontaneous speech (including that of children)'. In this view he is completely at odds with Chomsky (1965:31), who assumes that actual language is 'degenerate' and deviates from the rules of grammar.

It might also be argued that the treatment of language in terms of sentences has been quite successful in revealing how language works, that within the sentence we can establish rules and constraints concerning what is and is not allowed, whereas beyond the sentence, such rules seem either to disintegrate or turn into rules of a different kind—social rules or psychological rules, which are not within the area of linguistic study at all. So linguists too tend to come up with grammatically correct, but somewhat peculiar examples: 'Sincerity may frighten the boy' (Chomsky 1965:63) and so on.

All these arguments, from people involved in different ways in the study of language, have weight, and should not be ridiculed or dismissed out of hand, as has become rather fashionable in some language teaching circles. There are types of language use which demand the ability to formulate grammatical, correctly bounded sentences, and being able to exploit the formal sentence grammar is one of the most important elements in being able to communicate in a language. Yet if we *are* going to approach language as isolated artificially constructed sentences, even if only occasionally and for limited purposes, we do need to make a case for this, and not just do it because that is the tradition: in the mother tongue classroom, for the foreign language learner, or in linguistics. We should also recognize that there is more to producing and understanding meaningful language—to communicating—than knowing how to make or recognize correct sentences. A person who could do only that, and did so without any other considerations, would be, as the sociolinguist Dell Hymes (1971 [1972:277]) has said, 'likely to be institutionalised' for saying all kinds of inappropriate, irrelevant, and uninteresting things. Being a communicator, having what Hymes calls *communicative competence*, involves much more.

▶ TASK 2

Some of the following are invented examples, for language teaching or grammatical analysis, and some are pieces of language which were actually used to communicate. Is there any way of telling which is which? Can you think of situations where these pieces of language might actually have been used?

1 John considers the analyst a lunatic.
2 Which of you people is the fish?
3 Please don't throw me on the floor!
4 Cross since 1846.
5 I wish someone had told me he was vegetarian: I could have made an omelette.
6 Chicken and vegetable . . . hot . . . medium hot . . . er rice . . . pilao rice, er two poppadums and a . . . what's a bhindi bhaji?

1.3 Discourse and the sentence

We have, then, two different kinds of language as potential objects for study: one abstracted in order to teach a language or literacy, or to study how the rules of language work, and another which has been used to communicate something and is felt to be coherent (and may, or may not, happen to correspond to a correct sentence or a series of correct sentences). This latter kind of language—language in use, for communication—is called *discourse*; and the search for what gives discourse coherence is *discourse analysis*. It is important to notice that the distinction between these two kinds of language (the artificially constructed and the communicating) is often more a question of the way we use or think about a particular stretch of language, than the way it is in itself. It is possible to take a stretch of language which someone has used in communication and treat it as a sentence for a translation exercise, or an object for grammatical analysis. Conversely, it is possible to take a sentence from a language teaching or linguistics textbook, go to the country where the language is spoken, say it to someone in a suitable situation, and achieve something by saying it. (That is why, in Task 2, although one may make a pretty good guess on the basis of past experience, there is no sure way of knowing whether the sentences which are grammatically correct—like (1), (3), and (5)—have been used or just invented.) The two approaches are not mutually exclusive. Discourse may be composed of one or more well-formed grammatical sentences—and indeed it often is—but it does not have to be. It can have grammatical 'mistakes' in it, and often does. The British politician Geoffrey Howe said in an interview on television: 'We thought it was right to come to a decision when I next met them last night.' This worked as a part of the discourse he was involved in (the interview) even if he did use a grammatical construction which might well have got a red line through it if he had written it as part of a school essay. Discourse treats the rules of grammar as a resource, conforming to them when it needs to, but departing from them when it does not. It sometimes does the same with conventional meanings too. When a waiter asked me, and the people I was eating with, sentence (2) in Task 2, we understood him, even though, in textbook terms, his words might seem to be nonsense. Discourse can be anything from a grunt or single expletive, through short conversations and scribbled notes right up to Tolstoy's novel, *War and Peace*, or a lengthy legal case. What matters is not its conformity to rules, but the fact that it communicates and is recognized by its receivers as coherent. This leads us to the disturbing conclusion that there is a degree of subjectivity in identifying a stretch of language as discourse—it may be meaningful and thus communicate to one person in a way which another person does not have the necessary knowledge to make sense of—yet in practice we find that discourse is usually perceived as such by groups, rather than individuals.

1.4 Grammar within and beyond the sentence

Now for our second problem: how *did* you know that the second passage quoted in Task 1 was the beginning of a unified, meaningful stretch of language, while the first was just gobbledegook, randomly assembled without reason?

One possibility is that the kinds of rules which operate within sentences operate between them as well: that grammar, to put it another way, does not stop with a full stop but reaches over it. So just as, if I begin a sentence with 'The ...', there are rules which limit what word can follow it (I cannot, for example, continue 'The an ...' though I can continue 'The knight . . .'), perhaps there are also rules which limit what kind of sentence can follow another.

▶ TASK 3

Here is a well-formed 'correct', grammatical sentence:

The girls rode their motor-cycles through the corn.

Here are five versions which would usually be classed as incorrect. (Following convention, we use an asterisk * to indicate our belief that these examples are wrong.) What kind of mistakes do the sentences contain?

1 *The girl's rode their motor-cycles through the corn.
2 *The girls road there motor-cicles through the corn.
3 *The girls rided their motors-cycle through the corns.
4 *The corn through girls the rode motor-cycles their.
5 *The girls rode their houses through the corn.

Are we justified in regarding these examples as unequivocally wrong in all circumstances? Can you, for example, think of situations in which (3) and (5) would be acceptable? How far do the errors interfere with the original meaning?

Let us investigate this possibility that grammar extends beyond sentences. If we violate the internal rules of sentences we produce examples which would be dismissed as 'wrong'. (There are doubtful and borderline cases, but in practice most teachers, examiners, and linguists do act as though there are right and wrong sentences.) We can identify three kinds of sentence which are considered wrong, in addition to those with writing errors of spelling and punctuation.

Morphological errors: where the word endings (or other word parts) are wrong
*The knight kill a dragons.

Syntactic errors: where the word order is wrong
*The a knight dragon killed.

Semantic errors: where the meaning is wrong
*The knight killed a teaspoon.

Although in this last case we should note that it is much harder to talk of the sentence being 'wrong'; there are circumstances when people validly violate semantic norms, as we shall see.

In the same way that there are rules within sentences, limiting which words can follow others, so there might also be rules within discourses, limiting which sentence can follow another one, and if I write 'The knight killed the dragon', then there might be limits, or constraints, on what I can put as the next sentence. I might write:

The knight killed the dragon. He cut off its head with his sword.

and this would seem quite reasonable; but could I write this?

The knight killed the dragon. The pineapple was on the table.

It is unlikely, but it does not seem to be 'wrong' in quite the same way as the sentences in Task 3. Stretching our imaginations, we can surely create a story which might contain this sequence, just as we could, in fact, create fanciful circumstances in which knights kill teaspoons, and girls ride houses. Perhaps, in this fictional world (it must be fictional if it has dragons in it) the knight is seeking a magic pineapple, hoarded in a dragon's cave. He fears he is too late, and the pineapple will have gone. He kills the dragon, bursts into its cave, and sees that . . . In other words, the two sentences *might* go together, but the reasons are not strictly linguistic; they are to do with our knowledge of the world where these events take place (although that knowledge may also have come to us through language). The same is true for the opening of the detective novel in Task 1. We recognize it as a unified stretch of language because we know facts about novels, layout, publishers, telephones, being woken up, and so on.

So we now have two possible answers to the problem of how we recognize a stretch of language as unified and meaningful. One is that we employ language rules of the type studied by grammarians and taught in most language textbooks, and that these rules operate between sentences as well as within them. The other is that we employ knowledge—of the world, of the speaker, of social convention, of what is going on around us as we read or listen—in order to make sense of the language we are encountering. We shall return to the possibility of there being rules operating across sentence boundaries in detail in 2. Then in 3 to 6 we shall deal with the other possible answer: the way that coherence is created by factors outside language. But before we move on, it may be instructive to look at the relationship between language viewed as a formal system and language as part of a wider social and psychological context, and to say something about the place of these two approaches in the development of ideas about language in general.

1.5 Language in and out of context

When we receive a linguistic message, we pay attention to many other factors apart from the language itself. If we are face to face with the person sending the message, then we notice what they are doing with their face, eyes, and body while speaking: maybe they smiled, or shook their fist, or looked away. In a spoken message we notice the quality of the voice as well: maybe the speaker's voice was shaking, or they had a particular accent, or hesitated, or slurred their words. These are the *paralinguistic* features of a spoken message, which are lost if we write the message down. They exist in written messages too, where we may be influenced by handwriting or typography, and by whether the message is in an expensive book or on a scrap of paper.

We are also influenced by the situation in which we receive messages, by our cultural and social relationship with the participants, by what we know and what we assume the sender knows. These factors take us beyond the study of language, in a narrow sense, and force us to look at other areas of inquiry—the mind, the body, society, the physical world—in fact, at everything. There are good arguments for limiting a field of study to make it manageable; but it is also true to say that the answer to the question of what gives discourse its unity may be impossible to give without considering the world at large: the *context*.

In linguistics, especially in the English-speaking world between the 1930s and 1960s, there have been several schools of thought which believe that context—this knowledge of the world outside language which we use to interpret it—should be ruled out of language analysis as far as possible. In this way, it is believed, linguists will be able to make discoveries about the language itself, and its system of rules which exists quite independently of particular circumstances. Though there are variations of this view, and disagreements among its adherents, we may validly characterize it as *sentence linguistics*, because it confines its inquiries to what happens within sentences. Sentence linguists follow one of two procedures: they either invent their examples for analysis, using their own intuitive knowledge as native speakers (their *linguistic competence*) as a yardstick, or they take language which people have actually used and remove all the features which they believe to be irrelevant to their purposes. These processes, especially the first, are very similar to those used in creating practice sentences for language teaching.

This is best demonstrated by an example. A verbal exchange between two people was recorded and part of it was written down. Inevitably, this involves loss, because it is not possible to reproduce on the page all the features of voices, movements, expressions, and of the situation; but it is possible to keep or discard differing amounts. At one point the exchange went something like this:

A: Right, (.hhh) who's goin' to lift the bottom?
Well . . . come o' . . . someone's got to take 'old of it.
B: I ain't goin' to.
A: Don't jus' . . . Come on will you?

Without using any technical transcription system (the convention *.hhh* simply means a sharply indrawn breath) we can capture quite a lot of detail: *goin'* instead of *going*, *'old* instead of *hold*, *ain't* instead of *am not* all indicate a dialect other than that of standard English. *O'* indicates the word *on* broken off. Though it is unfinished, the false start *Don't jus'* . . . has meaning and perhaps suggests a sense of urgency and impatience. Yet sentence linguists would regard these features as unimportant: their objective being to analyse the rules of the English language, not the actual meanings which **A** and **B** are trying to convey in this particular situation, nor their departures from the standard form of the language. They would also omit any individual idiosyncrasies in an individual's language (known in linguistics as *idiolect*), and any purely physiological interference, like traffic noise outside or the effect of trying to speak while under physical strain. Lastly, they would remove what is undoubtedly, in the case above, the single most important feature needed to understand what is being said: the fact that these two people are involved in moving a piano and **A** (a middle-aged man trying to assert his authority) is already supporting its weight: hence, perhaps, his impatience, breathlessness, and desperate switch from ordering to pleading with **B**, a youth who has only reluctantly agreed to come along and help. (It is worth noting that titles of discourses often supply a broad explanatory context; we might, for example, have called this extract 'The Piano Movers', and immediately made it much more meaningful by doing so.) By removing these sorts of features— hesitations, false starts, social or regional dialects, idiolect, interference, what people are doing and who they are—sentence linguists would argue that we take away what is incidental and variable in language and leave what is permanent and invariable. They might render the same exchange like this:

A: Who is going to lift the bottom?
Someone has got to take hold of it.

B: I am not going to.

A: Come on, will you?

Interestingly, this process of eliminating the unique combination of circumstances in which language happens (a process known technically as *idealization*) results in the same kind of sentences as those invented examples for translation or grammatical analysis which we looked at in **1.2.** For their purposes, the sentence linguists have a case. Yet for the discourse analyst it may be exactly these transient and variable features which enable us to understand the meaning of what is said, and the reason why the order of sentences proceeds in the way that it does. The language learner needs to be able to handle language which is not idealized— language in use. The language teacher needs, therefore, to decide on the extent to which idealized language may help the development of this ability.

▶ ## TASK 4

Here is a transcript of a conversation. What additional information do you need to make sense of it?

A: That blonde girl over the road there . . . Careful don't bang your head . . . Sometimes she looks . . .

B: What? Which one? Ow!

A: I said to you don't bang your head. Sometimes she looks quite pretty, sometimes she looks quite ugly.

B: I'm OK, leave me alone.

We have, then, two approaches to language: sentence linguistics and discourse analysis. It is not a question of setting these two up as irreconcilable enemies, trying to make one a hero and the other a villain, for both have an invaluable contribution to make to the understanding of language, and both ultimately need each other. The distinction, though convenient for us at the moment, is not absolute, and just as we cannot communicate with *only* the rules of semantics and grammar, so we just as surely cannot communicate very well without them. Leaving this aside for the moment though, let us set up a contrast between the two as follows:

Sentence linguistics data	*Discourse analysis data*
Isolated sentences	Any stretch of language felt to be unified
Grammatically well-formed	Achieving meaning
Without context	In context
Invented or idealized	Observed

1.6 The origins of discourse analysis

If we accept this division between two different approaches to the search for order and regularity in language, it is not accurate to regard the second, discourse analysis, as something totally new, without any kind of pedigree in the language study of the past. The first known students of language in the Western tradition, the scholars of Greece and Rome, were aware of these different approaches too, and divided grammar from rhetoric, the former being concerned with the rules of language as an isolated object, the latter with how to do things with words, to achieve effects, and communicate successfully with people in particular contexts. Ironically, some schools of discourse analysis—often thought of as one of the newest disciplines of language study—employ terms from classical rhetoric, one of the oldest. And there have always been, throughout history, studies of language in context, under various guises. In twentieth-century linguistics, alongside sentence linguistics, there have also been influential approaches which studied language in its full context, as part of society and the world. In North America, in the early decades of this century, exciting work on language was conducted by people, who were at once both anthropologists and linguists (and are claimed by both disciplines), often involved in research into the languages and societies of the native Americans (Indians). In Britain a similar tradition developed in the work of J. R. Firth, who saw language, not as an autonomous system, but as part of a culture, which is in turn responsive to the environment. These traditions (together with others outside the English-speaking world) have plenty of insights to offer to discourse analysis. In addition, there are many other disciplines—

philosophy, psychology and psychiatry, sociology and anthropology, Artificial Intelligence, media studies, literary studies—which often examine their object of study—the mind, society, other cultures, computers, the media, works of literature—through language, and are thus carrying out their own discourse analysis, very often some of the best. This entanglement of different disciplines can be very confusing, and seems to suggest that discourse analysis is not really a separate activity at all, but a pursuit in danger of evaporating into others. Perhaps the most useful distinction is to think of other disciplines as studying something else through discourse; whereas discourse analysis has discourse as its prime object of study, and though it may take excursions into many different fields, must always be careful to return to the main concern.

Ironically, it was a sentence linguist who both coined the term 'discourse analysis' and initiated a search for language rules which would explain how sentences were connected within a text by a kind of extended grammar. This was Zellig Harris. In 1952, in an article entitled 'Discourse Analysis', he analysed an advertisement for hair tonic—from which he coyly omitted the brand name—and set about searching for grammatical rules to explain why one sentence followed another. (Luckily for him, each sentence in the advertisement was grammatically well formed.) The details of his analysis need not concern us; but his conclusions are extremely interesting. At the beginning of the article he observed that there were two possible directions for discourse analysis. One was 'continuing descriptive Linguistics beyond the limits of a single sentence at a time' (Harris 1952 [1964:356]). This was what he aimed to achieve. The other was 'correlating culture and language (i.e. non-linguistic and linguistic behaviour)' (loc. cit.). Being a sentence linguist, this was something he did not regard as his concern. But having weighed up the two options, at the end of the article, he concluded: '. . . in every language it turns out that almost all the results lie within a relatively short stretch which we may call the sentence . . . Only rarely can we state restrictions across sentences' (loc. cit.).

If we are to find the answer to the problem of what gives stretches of language unity and meaning, we must look beyond the formal rules operating within sentences, and consider the people who use language, and the world in which it happens as well. Yet before we do so, it would be as well to see just how far formal, purely linguistic rules *can* go in accounting for the way one sentence succeeds another. This will be our next area of inquiry.

2 Formal links

2.1 Formal and contextual links

We have seen how our feeling that a particular stretch of language in some way *hangs together*, or *has unity*, (that it is, in other words, discourse), cannot be accounted for in the same way as our feeling for the acceptability of a sentence. In order to account for discourse, we need to look at features outside the language: at the situation, the people involved, what they know and what they are doing. These facts enable us to construct stretches of language as discourse; as having a meaning and a unity for us. The way we recognize correct and incorrect sentences is different. We can do this through our knowledge of grammar without reference to outside facts.

We can describe the two ways of approaching language as *contextual*, referring to facts outside language, and *formal*, referring to facts inside language. A way of understanding this difference may be to think of formal features as in some way built up in our minds from the black marks which form writing on the page, or from the speech sounds picked up by our ears, while contextual features are somewhere outside this physical realization of the language—in the world, or pre-existing in the minds of the participants. Stretches of language treated only formally are referred to as *text*.

Now although it is true that we need to consider contextual factors to explain what it is that creates a feeling of unity in stretches of language of more than one sentence, we cannot say that there are *no* formal links between sentences in discourse. There are some, as we shall see, and although language teaching and mainstream linguistics has traditionally concentrated only upon those formal features which operate within sentences, discourse analysis may suggest ways of directing teachers' and students' attention to formal features which operate across sentences as well. We shall now try to categorize these formal links and then examine how far they will go in helping to explain why a succession of sentences is discourse, and not just a disconnected jumble.

Formal links between sentences and between clauses are known as *cohesive devices* and they can be dealt with under the headings in **2.2** to **2.8**.

2.2 Verb form

The form of the verb in one sentence can limit the choice of the verb form in the next, and we may be justified in saying that a verb form in one sentence is 'wrong', or at least 'unlikely', because it does not fit with the form in another. If we look back at the exchange between the piano movers, for example, we can see that the verbs (*'s goin, 's got to take, ain't goin', don't, come on*) are all in the present (although they refer to the future). There seems to be a degree of formal connection between them, a way in which the first tense conditions all the others, and it would be very strange if the exchange had been:

A: Right, who's goin' to lift the bottom?
      Well, someone had got to take hold of it.

B: I shan't have been goin' to.

A: Don't . . . Come on will you?

2.3 Parallelism

▶ TASK 5

What links are there between sentences in the following?

He vastly enriched the world by his inventions. He enriched the field of knowledge by his teaching. He enriched humanity by his precepts and his personal example. He died on December 17, 1907, and was buried in Westminster Abbey with the honours due to a prince of men . . .
(Arthur Mee (ed.): *Immortal Heroes of the World*)

Another link within discourse is effected by *parallelism*, a device which suggests a connection, simply because the form of one sentence or clause repeats the form of another. This is often used in speeches, prayers, poetry, and advertisements. It can have a powerful emotional effect, and it is also a useful *aide-mémoire*. Here, for example, is part of a Christian prayer:

'Teach us, Good Lord, to give and not to count the cost, to fight and not to heed the wounds, to toil and not to seek for rest, to labour and to ask for no reward, save that of knowing that we do Thy will.' (*St Richard's Prayer*)

Here the discourse proceeds through a repeated grammatical structure (*to X and not to Y the/for Z*) into which different words are slotted, creating a rhythm which is finally broken in the last phrase in a way which may seem to imitate the sense of relief and reward the prayer concerns. (In a secondary school where this was regularly used in morning prayers it had to be abandoned because the pupils exploited the rhythm created by the parallelism to make it sound like a football chant!) This example employs parallelism to link clauses, but the same principle is used to link sentences too. A televised address to the French people by President Pompidou began:

'Le Général de Gaulle est mort. La France est veuve.' (General de Gaulle is dead. France is a widow.)

Here the two sentences are linked because they follow the grammatical pattern, *definite article + proper noun + copula + complement,* a link whose purely formal nature is revealed by the fact that it does not really survive translation into English, where the definite articles are not needed and an indefinite one is. In French the two sentences are further linked by the contrasted masculine and feminine genders reinforcing the metaphor of deceased husband and bereaved wife.

Parallelism, which suggests a connection of meaning through an echo of form, does not have to be grammatical parallelism. It may be a *sound parallelism*: as in the rhyme, rhythm, and other sound effects of verse. One might even extend the idea and talk of *semantic parallelism* where two sentences are linked because they mean the same thing. Comic duos often exploit this for humorous effect. The first comedian says something in a high-flown style, and the other repeats the same information in a colloquial one:

A: The Good Lord, in his wisdom, has taken her away from us.

B: You mean the old girl's snuffed it.

2.4 Referring expressions

These are words whose meaning can only be discovered by referring to other words or to elements of the context which are clear to both sender and receiver. The most obvious example of them is third person pronouns (*she/her/hers/herself*; *he/him/his/himself*; *it/its/itself*; *they/them/their/ theirs/themselves*). If we are listening to a story and somebody says *So I ate it* we may well know the meaning of *it* from somewhere earlier in the story. We choose the most likely meaning for *it* from the text. It is important to notice that our knowledge of the meaning of *it* is only partly formal though. It involves our knowledge of the world as well, and if the story had gone

There was a pineapple on the table. So I ate it.

we would assume the speaker had eaten the pineapple, not the table (even though the word *table* is nearer) because we know that people are more likely to eat pineapples than tables. A computer would have to be given knowledge about human eating habits before it could interpret this. There are extraordinary cases, however, and in a story anything can happen, even the digestion of tables.

In an extended piece of discourse, a common procedure, known as *anaphora*, is for the identity of someone or something to be given once at the beginning, and thereafter referred to as *she* or *he* or *it*. This makes a kind of chain, running through the discourse, in which each expression is linked to another:

a pineapple . . . it . . . it . . . it . . .

It is not only third person pronouns which work in this way. The meanings of *this* and *that*, and *here* and *there* have also to be found either formally in another part of the discourse or contextually from the world.

The meaning of a referring expression is not always in another sentence or clause, of course. If two people arrive at the door with a piano and say:

Where shall we put it?

we can assume that *it* means the piano. We choose the most likely meaning for *it* from the world, and in this case the meaning is contextual. One of the people with the piano might have had a pencil between their teeth, but would probably have been annoyed if we had taken *it* to mean the pencil and said:

Put it on the mantelpiece.

Sometimes people assume that the meaning of a pronoun is clear when it is not. Then there are misunderstandings, and we have to say:

Not the pencil, you idiot, the piano!

Foreign language teachers, assuming that comprehension difficulties arise from new vocabulary, can overlook the difficulties students can have in interpreting the meaning of referring expressions within discourse.

▶   TASK 6

Look at this opening section of a children's book:

Here is Edward Bear, coming downstairs now, bump, bump, bump, on the back of his head, behind Christopher Robin. It is, as far as he knows, the only way of coming downstairs, but sometimes he feels that there really is another way, if only he could stop bumping for a moment and think of it. And then he feels that perhaps there isn't. Anyhow, here he is at the bottom, and ready to be introduced to you. Winnie-the-Pooh.
   When I first heard his name, I said, just as you are going to say, 'But I thought he was a boy?'
(A. A. Milne: *Winnie-the-Pooh*)

Identify the referring expressions, and the word(s) they refer back to. Are there any doubtful cases, and how do you resolve them? (How do you know whether *he* refers to Pooh or Christopher Robin? What does the first word *Here* mean?)

It is not always as simple as following the chain back until we come to a name or a noun. Even in a passage as deceptively childlike as this, there are several more complex examples. *Here* refers either to an imaginary situation or to the picture on the facing page, which shows Pooh coming downstairs. *It* at the beginning of the second sentence refers to *coming downstairs* (and not to *his head*, of course), and then the next *it* refers to *another way*. The next *here* refers to a new imaginary situation. *I* is the author, and *you* is the reader—although here a trick is played and the author talks to us as though we are there, listening rather than reading. This story is written to be read out loud, and in many contemporary cultures, reading out loud is something done mostly for children. That, together with the subject matter, accounts for our feeling at this point that the story is being sent to a child, the *you*. So we can see how complicated this network of referring expressions is, and how skilled even quite young children are at understanding it. Yet if, as teachers, we concentrate our attention on formal links within sentences, we are taking all these skills for granted, and may leave our students completely at sea.

▶   TASK 7

Here is another chapter opening from the same children's book. What is different about the use of the pronouns?

Nobody seemed to know where they came from, but there they were in the Forest: Kanga and Baby Roo.
(A. A. Milne: *Winnie-the-Pooh*, Chapter 7)

Sometimes the chain has to be followed in the opposite direction. We are given the pronoun first, and then kept in suspense as to its identity, which is revealed later. This is known as *cataphora*, and it is a favourite opening device of authors who begin stories and novels with an unidentified *he* or *she*, both enticing us to look further, and plunging us into the middle of a situation as though we already knew what was going on. Again, this device seems to be one which children can handle quite early, if Task 7 is a good indicator.

Referring expressions fulfil a dual purpose of unifying the text (they depend upon some of the subject matter remaining the same) and of economy, because they save us from having to repeat the identity of what we are talking about again and again.

2.5 Repetition and lexical chains

▶ TASK 8

1 Timotei is both mild to your hair and to your scalp—so mild you
  can wash your hair as often as you like. Timotei cleans your hair
  gently, leaving it soft and shiny, with a fresh smell of summer
  meadows.

2 This Schedule and Policy shall be read together as one contract
  and any word or expression to which a specific meaning has been
  attached in any part of the said Schedule or Policy shall bear such
  specific meaning wherever the word or expression may appear.

Both these extracts avoid referring expressions. Why? Would it
make any difference if the second extract was rewritten with
referring expressions instead of repetition? Can you think of other
discourse types which often avoid referring expressions, and, if so,
what are the reasons for this?

Repetition of words can create the same sort of chain as pronouns, and
there are sometimes good reasons for preferring it. In Britain, mother
tongue learners of English are discouraged from using repetition on the
grounds that it is 'bad style', and encouraged to use a device known as
'elegant repetition', where synonymous or more general words or phrases
are used. So instead of writing

The pineapple . . . the pineapple . . . the pineapple . . . the pineapple

they might write

The pineapple . . . the luscious fruit . . . our meal . . . the tropical luxury

The kind of link that we choose will depend upon the kind of discourse we
are seeking to create, and elegant repetition is not always desirable. It may
sound pretentious in casual conversation, or create dangerous ambiguity in
a legal document (though this view of legal discourse can be challenged). As
teachers, we need to sensitize students to the interplay of discourse type and
the choice between referring expressions, repetition, and elegant repetition.

▶ TASK 9

In the following, is it possible or desirable to

1 replace repetitions with referring expressions
2 replace referring expressions by repetitions
3 replace either by elegant repetition

and, if so, would this affect the meaning, the style, or both? What
does *all this* refer to in the third sentence?

Hold the disc by its labelled end, with the side you wish to use to the left. Now insert the disc into the drive slot until it clicks home. All this should require no more than gentle pressure: if the drive appears to be resisting the disc, stop. Whatever you do, don't force it. The other thing to remember is that you can damage your discs by inserting them before switching the computer on, or for that matter by leaving them in while you switch it off.
(*Amstrad PCW8256 User Guide*)

We have described referring expressions, repetition, and elegant repetition as establishing 'chains' of connected words running through discourse. Such *lexical chains* need not necessarily consist of words which mean the same, however. They may also be created by words which associate with each other. This association may be by virtue of some formal semantic connection (*good*, for example, associates with its opposite *bad*; *animal* with any example of an animal like *horse*; *violin* with *orchestra* of which it is a part), or it may be because words are felt to belong to some more vaguely defined lexical group (*rock star*; *world tour*; *millionaire*; *yacht*). This last kind of connection, though it is sometimes treated as a kind of cohesion (Halliday and Hasan 1976:284–7), is really too dependent upon individual experience and knowledge to be treated as a formal link. We shall return to it under another heading in **6**.

2.6 Substitution

Another kind of formal link between sentences is the *substitution* of words like *do* or *so* for a word or group of words which have appeared in an earlier sentence. It would be very long-winded if we had always to answer a question like *Do you like mangoes?* with a sentence like *Yes I like mangoes* or *Yes I think I like mangoes*. It is much quicker, and it means the same, if we say *Yes I do* or *Yes I think so*. Unfortunately, much traditional language teaching, in its zeal for practising verb tenses and using new vocabulary, has concentrated exclusively on longer forms (*Answer with a full sentence please!*) and deprived students of briefer, more authentic options.

2.7 Ellipsis

Sometimes we do not even need to provide a substitute for a word or phrase which has already been said. We can simply omit it, and know that the missing part can be reconstructed quite successfully. Instead of answering *Would you like a glass of beer?* with *Yes I would like a glass of beer* we can just say *Yes I would* knowing that *like a glass of beer* will be understood. Or if someone says *What are you doing?* we can just answer *Eating a mango* instead of *I am eating a mango* because we know that *I am* is understood and does not have to be said. Omitting part of sentences on the assumption that an earlier sentence or the context will make the meaning clear is known as *ellipsis*.

▶ TASK 10

Look at Tasks 5–9 again, and find any instances of substitution or ellipsis.

2.8 Conjunction

Yet another type of formal relation between sentences—and perhaps the most apparent—is provided by those words and phrases which explicitly draw attention to the type of relationship which exists between one sentence or clause and another. These are *conjunctions*. These words may simply add more information to what has already been said (*and, furthermore, add to that*) or elaborate or exemplify it (*for instance, thus, in other words*). They may contrast new information with old information, or put another side to the argument (*or, on the other hand, however, conversely*). They may relate new information to what has already been given in terms of causes (*so, consequently, because, for this reason*) or in time (*formerly, then, in the end, next*) or they may indicate a new departure or a summary (*by the way, well, to sum up, anyway*). There are many words and phrases which can be put into this category in English, and many different ways in which they can be classified. They indicate the relationship of utterances in the mind or in the world and are thus in a way contextual. Language learners need to know both how and when to use them. Their presence or absence in discourse often contributes to style, and some conjunctions can sound very pompous when used inappropriately.

2.9 Conclusion

We now have a means of assessing the extent of formal links within a piece of discourse. In **3** we shall see that these links are neither necessary nor sufficient to account for our sense of the unity of discourse. Their presence does not automatically make a passage coherent, and their absence does not automatically make it meaningless.

As teachers, we should notice that a clear understanding of the formal connections between sentences may help to explain one of the ways in which foreign language students sometimes write supposedly connected sentences, each of which is well-formed in itself, but which somehow add up to very strange discourse. It can also help us to identify why a student is not achieving the stylistic effect he or she is seeking. It should be clear that the correctness and the effect of some expressions cannot only be judged within the sentence, but must be judged in connection with other sentences in the discourse as well. We shall return to the question of how awareness of cohesive devices may affect teaching practice in **11** and **13**.

▶ TASK 11

Identify and categorize all the formal links which connect the three sentences in the following invented dialogue:

A: It's a mystery to me, how the conjuror sawed that woman in half.

B: Well, Jane was the woman he did it to. So presumably she must know.

3   Why formal links are not enough

3.1 Introduction

It is important to realize that although formal links reinforce the unity of discourse, they cannot, on their own, create it. The sentences in Task 11 are packed with cohesive devices, but it would be a mistake to suppose that it is this, and nothing else, which creates the unity between them. We can see this clearly if we replace the third sentence with another, so that the sequence reads:

A: It's a mystery to me, how the conjuror sawed that woman in half.
B: Well, Jane was the woman he did it to. So presumably she must be Japanese.

Here, there are also formal links (*So, she*, etc.) but it is not clear how the sequence makes sense. Of course, like the sentences about the knight, the dragon, and the pineapple, they *might* form part of a discourse, and if we stretch our imaginations we could come up with a situation in which they do; but this will not be by virtue of the words *so* and *she*, but because of some other information about the context.

Formal links between sentences, then, are not enough to account for our feeling that a stretch of language is discourse. They are neither necessary nor sufficient, and in brief spoken exchanges, it is quite common to encounter sequences of sentences that are almost entirely bare of them.

▶   TASK 12

Here are four possible answers to the sentence: 'The window is open.'

1 Go back to sleep, will you?
2 Don't worry.
3 My job's stacking boxes, mate.
4 By Jove, Holmes! It was the gardener!

For each exchange, supply a context in which it would make sense. Notice that there are no formal links in any of the exchanges, but they are nevertheless easy to understand. Each one could form a complete discourse.

3.2 Language functions

The examples in Task 12 are invented; but one does not have to look far to find such exchanges in real life. An elderly neighbour came to my door one day and said: 'Sorry, love. I saw you were home. There's a cat stuck under the gate at number 67.' I had no trouble in interpreting this, nor did I find the sequence strange, despite the fact that there are no overt formal links of the kind discussed in **2**. Clearly, if we are to explain such interpretation we will need more than our list of cohesive devices.

One way of doing this is to look behind the literal, formal meaning of what is said or written, and to consider what the sender of a message intends to achieve with it, to try to understand its *function*. People are interpreting other people's language—and expecting other people to interpret their own—in this way all the time, apparently with a surprising degree of accuracy. In the above example, the old woman at the door intended to establish contact, apologize for disturbing me, explain why she had come to my house instead of another, and ask for assistance in freeing the cat. That I correctly interpreted this is strongly suggested by the fact that she was not surprised by my answer—which was to stop what I was doing, go out with her, and set about trying to free the cat. If I had simply interpreted her remarks as having the function of imparting information and replied: 'Oh, how interesting. Thanks for telling me', she would, quite justifiably, have been very offended. But how could she be so certain that her intention would be transparent to me, and how did I understand her meaning so accurately? What kind of rules enable people to infer the function of what is said from its literal, formal meaning?

In order to discover how such inferences are made, we will need firstly to examine the range of possible functions of language, and secondly to try to understand how people correctly interpret them. Understanding this connection between the form and the function of language will help us to explain how stretches of language, like the request for help with the cat, can be coherent without being cohesive; it will also help us as language teachers. We cannot assume that these interpretations will be made in the same way in all cultures and in all languages, so understanding how interpretation proceeds in the culture of the language we are teaching is crucial if we are to help foreign learners to make their words function in the way that they intend.

From now on, we shall use the term *utterance* for a unit of language used by somebody in context to do something—to communicate—and reserve *sentence* for grammatically complete units regarded purely formally, in isolation from their context and their function.

3.3 The classification of macro-functions

Specialists in linguistics sometimes claim that if non-specialists are asked what the function of language is, they will reply that it is 'to send information' or 'to tell other people your thoughts'. People are not as simplistic as this; even a moment's reflection leads to the conclusion that language has many more functions. Nevertheless it is true, in the adult and public world at least, that this function which language has of transmitting information, its *referential* function, is considered the most important. To abuse it, by sending false information, is usually regarded as wrong, and can, in certain circumstances, incur the punishment of imprisonment or a fine. Yet it is by no means the only, or the first, function of language in human life. In the world of the infant and parent, the referential function of language often takes a subordinate role to others. There is little the four-year-old child can tell his or her parents that they do not know already, for they share the child's world almost entirely. The same is true in other intimate relationships. Some conversations of couples, whether affectionate or belligerent, have scant informational content. And even in the wider social world of adult intercourse, language clearly has many more functions than simply sending information.

▶ TASK 13

You hear one side of a telephone call in a foreign language. The speaker says: 'tak . . . tak . . . nu da . . . tak . . . pravda? . . . tak . . .'. What do you think the function of these words is and what are their English equivalents?

There have been many, sometimes conflicting, attempts to classify the main functions of language (*macro-functions*). One of the clearest and most influential was formulated by the linguist Roman Jakobson (1960), and further developed by Dell Hymes (1962). (The terms we shall use here are based on both accounts, without exactly following either.) The scheme proceeds by first identifying the elements of communication, as follows:

The addresser: the person who originates the message. This is usually the same as the person who is sending the message, but not always, as in the case of messengers, spokespeople, and town criers.
The addressee: the person to whom the message is addressed. This is usually the person who receives the message, but not necessarily so, as in the case of intercepted letters, bugged telephone calls, and eavesdropping.
The channel: the medium through which the message travels: sound waves, marks on paper, telephone wires, word processor screens.
The message form: the particular grammatical and lexical choices of the message.
The topic: the information carried in the message.
The code: the language or dialect, for example, Swedish, Yorkshire English, Semaphore, British Sign Language, Japanese.
The setting: the social or physical context.

Macro-functions are then established, each focusing attention upon one element:

The emotive function: communicating the inner states and emotions of the addresser ('Oh no!', 'Fantastic!', 'Ugh!', and swear words used as exclamations).

The directive function: seeking to affect the behaviour of the addressee ('Please help me!', 'Shut up!', 'I'm warning you!').

The phatic function: opening the channel or checking that it is working, either for social reasons ('Hello', 'Lovely weather', 'Do you come here often?'), or for practical ones ('Can you hear me?', 'Are you still there?', 'Can you see the blackboard from the back of the room?', 'Can you read my writing?').

The poetic function: in which the particular form chosen is the essence of the message. (The advertising slogan *BEANZ MEANZ HEINZ* would lose its point if it were paraphrased as 'If you are buying beans, you will naturally buy Heinz.')

The referential function: carrying information.

The metalinguistic function: focusing attention upon the code itself, to clarify it or renegotiate it ('What does this word here mean?', 'This bone is known as the "femur"', '"Will" and "shall" mean the same thing nowadays'). This book has a largely metalinguistic function.

The contextual function: creating a particular kind of communication ('Right, let's start the lecture', 'It's just a game').

▶ ## TASK 14

What do you consider to be the most likely functions of the following?

1 Dear Sir or Madam . . .
2 Fred Astaire's dead.
3 Workers of the World, Unite!
4 You make me sick.
5 The court is now in session.
6 What do you mean by this?
7 Well, I'll be damned!
8 Here's Miss Julie.

Is it possible to assign one function to each, or are some of mixed function? How might the function of each utterance vary according to context?

3.4 Functional development

It is interesting to speculate, if one accepts this classification, on the evolution of functions in each human individual. The crying baby is being expressive, although her cries are not really language at all, but instinctive reactions to the environment. When she realizes that by controlling these cries, and producing them at will rather than automatically, she can influence the behaviour of her parents, she has progressed to the directive function. Phatic communication also begins very early. Chuckling, gurgling, babbling, often have no function but to say: 'Here I am, and so are you' (Halliday 1975:37–41). The poetic function is also apparent at an early stage: when young children latch on to a phrase and repeat it endlessly, without conveying any information. The referential function gains its prominence only at a later stage, and the metalinguistic function also comes later; these are the functions on which a considerable amount of attention is lavished at school.

Surprisingly, considering this course of development, a good deal of foreign language teaching begins with the metalinguistic function, by explicitly stating the rules of grammar.

3.5 Micro-functions and functional language teaching

If we accept Jakobson's and Hymes', or any similar, categorization of language into a small number of macro-functions, we might then go on to subdivide each function and specify more delicate categories, or *micro-functions*. A breakdown of the directive function, for example, might look something like Figure 1.

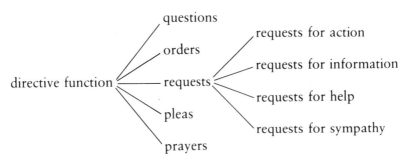

Figure 1

Figure 1 follows through only one function in each column, but one might easily imagine a similar division and re-division of any of the other six macro-functions, or of any of the resulting sub-categories. The result would be a diagram which becomes ever more precise and explicit as it moves from left to right, with a long list of fairly narrowly defined functions on the right-hand side. The resulting list of functions is of the kind used as the basis of functional language courses—the ones which use the term in any meaningful way rather than because it was fashionable—and this is the connection between functional courses and functional approaches to linguistics.

Functional courses set out to list the purposes for which students might wish to use language, and then to teach them how to do so. In this, they have important strengths, and they can teach students skills which courses concentrating on formal features of language often omit: how to greet people, or how to maintain polite contact while listening on the telephone. But they also have certain weaknesses, for the more exact one tries to become about functions, the more slippery they become, and the more scope there is for variation and disagreement. Certainly no list could ever claim to be exhaustive and complete. There are also pedagogic problems in following lists of functions through. What order should one follow? Are some functions more important than others? How exactly do they relate to grammar and vocabulary? We shall be returning to the treatment of functions in language teaching in Section Two.

3.6 Functional analysis and coherence

In **1** we set ourselves the problem of accounting for intuitions that some stretches of language are coherent and others are not. In **2** we examined the role of cohesive devices in creating coherence, but we also looked at their limitations. The idea of language function can go a long way towards solving this problem of what binds utterances together as discourse in the absence of formal links. If we can ascertain the function of utterances, we will be able to perceive a unity of a different kind. Thus we can see that the sentence 'The window is open' can have many different functions, depending on who says it, to whom, and in what situation. Said by a husband to a wife in the middle of the night it might function as an expression of worry. Said by a headteacher to a pupil it might well function as an order. Said by Sherlock Holmes to Dr Watson at the scene of a murder it might function as an interpretation. The same sentence is now seen to *do* different things, and according to what it is doing, the answer is more or less suitable:

The window is open.   →   Don't worry.
(*Expression of anxiety*)   →   (*Reassurance*)

There may be some kind of sequencing to functions, some order in the way they follow another: *request → refusal*; *plea → offer* and so on. This is not only the case when a discourse is constructed by two people interacting face to face; it may also hold within the words of a single speaker. My neighbour's utterances may follow more coherently if we construe them thus:

Sorry, love.   I saw you were home.   There's a cat stuck under the gate...
(*Apology*)   (*Explanation*)   (*Request*)

There are problems with this procedure, for not all functions can be so neatly labelled, nor is there always such a neat correspondence between a single utterance and a single function. As we have seen in Task 14, it is quite usual for an utterance to perform more than one function at once. Nor have we really explained our feeling for these sequences: why an order is more appropriately followed by a refusal than by a reassurance, for example. Nevertheless, the important principle has been established, that meaning varies with context. Formally, out of context, a sentence has a kind of time-free and place-free meaning. Used as an utterance in context it may have many meanings, which, although they are connected to this context-free sentence meaning, may be extremely varied.

These two types of meaning are distinguished by the terms *semantic* meaning (the fixed context-free meaning) and *pragmatic* meaning (the meaning which the words take on in a particular context, between particular people). The function of an utterance must be established pragmatically.

We are left, however, with two unanswered questions about the divergence of function and form, of semantics and pragmatics: How? and Why? If the meaning of an utterance does not wholly reside in the semantic meaning, and if people can mean quite different things with the same words, how do human beings interpret—usually quite accurately—what is meant from what is said? And why does this divergence of function and form exist at all? Why do people not just speak directly and say what they mean? For an answer we will need to look elsewhere: at the theories of conversational principles and speech acts, ideas which, as their names suggest, were developed with spoken language in mind, but are as applicable to written discourse as to spoken.

Examining these theories from pragmatics will involve us in a substantial digression from our main concern: which is to account for our intuitions of coherence and thus gain insight into the needs of the language learner, who after all aims to be able to produce coherent discourse, not isolated sentences. Yet these theories provide essential insights both into the nature of coherence, and into the problems of communicating in a foreign language and culture. They are essential tools for discourse analysis and thus for the teacher and learner.

3.7 Conversational principles: co-operation

The idea that conversation proceeds according to a principle, known and applied by all human beings, was first proposed in a limited form by the philosopher Paul Grice (1975), who put forward what he described as the *co-operative principle*. According to this principle, we interpret language on the assumption that its sender is obeying four maxims. We assume he or she is intending to:

- be true (*the maxim of quality*)
- be brief (*the maxim of quantity*)
- be relevant (*the maxim of relevance*)
- be clear (*the maxim of manner*)

Using this assumption, combined with general knowledge of the world, the receiver can reason from the literal, semantic meaning of what is said to the pragmatic meaning—and induce what the sender is intending to do with his or her words. For example: in the case of my neighbour's utterance that

There's a cat stuck under the gate at number 67

I started with the knowledge, from my experience of the world, that a cat is likely to be very unhappy at being stuck under a gate; that a human, by virtue of greater intelligence and manual dexterity is likely to be able to free such a cat; that humans generally like to alleviate the suffering of pets; and that old women in British society have an—often misplaced—belief in the practical abilities of men. From the co-operative principle, I also assumed that my neighbour was telling the truth (there was no evidence that she was lying, hallucinating, or playing a practical joke). I also assumed she was being relevant. If she had come and said, 'There's a flower growing in the garden at number 67', though this would also be true, it would be hard to see its relevance. Taking all this into account, it is possible to explain how I interpreted this utterance to function as a request for help in freeing the cat—as having a pragmatic meaning roughly paraphrasable as

Come and free the cat which is stuck under the gate at number 67.

If we also assume that my neighbour assumed that I knew these facts about the world, and that I interpreted her words according to the co-operative principle, then we can also see why the way she actually phrased her request is not only true and relevant, but also brief and clear. That I did in fact think this way, and that her assumptions about my assumptions were in fact correct, is borne out by the fact that I interpreted her words quickly, and that she seemed perfectly satisfied with my interpretation.

▶ # TASK 15

Look again at the exchanges in Task 12, and at the contexts you invented for them. How might the second speaker reason from the literal semantic meaning of 'The window is open' to its particular pragmatic function in context?

When we talk about people following the co-operative principle, this does not mean that they can consciously and explicitly formulate it to themselves. (If that were the case, then Grice's theory would not have attracted the attention it has!) It means rather that people act *as though* they know the principle just as they act *as though* they know the rules of grammar—though very few people can even begin to formulate them, and nobody can formulate them completely.

In the case of the trapped cat, my neighbour was able to obey all four maxims at once, and on the assumption that all four were in operation, I was able to correctly interpret what she said. But there are cases, when the demands of the four maxims do not fit so happily together. Asked 'What does your new job involve?' or 'Did you like Algeria?' it is difficult to obey both the quality maxim and the quantity maxim. Brevity and truth often pull in opposite directions, and the short answer is often simplified to the point of distortion. 'Water boils at 100° centigrade' is brief and considered to be true, but is it as true—if one can talk in degrees of truth—as the longer 'Water boils at different temperatures depending on altitude'? Legal discourse and scientific discourse often sacrifice the maxim of quantity to the maxim of quality. The maxims of quantity and manner are often at odds too. To be clear one sometimes needs to be long-winded.

3.8 Flouting the co-operative principle

There are also times when meaning derives from deliberate violations—or 'floutings' as Grice calls them—of the co-operative principle, always provided that the sender intends the receiver to perceive them as such, and that this is how, in fact, the receiver does perceive them. If the sender does not intend violations of the principle to be perceived as such, or if the receiver does not realize that they are deliberate, then communication degenerates into lying, obfuscation, or simply breaks down altogether. It is possible, for example, to flout the quality maxim without lying. If I tell you that

I've got millions of beer bottles in my cellar, or
My car breaks down every five minutes

though neither is literally true, you will perceive such remarks as figures of speech, hyperbole, a way of making my point more forcefully, rather than as lies. The same holds for metaphor ('Queen Victoria was made of iron') and irony and sarcasm ('I love it when you sing out of key all the time'), which depend upon the assumption that they will be interpreted as deliberate floutings of the charge to 'Be true' rather than as untruths intended to deceive. Note the importance, in all that has been said so far, of the sender's correct estimation of the receiver's state of knowledge. These figures of speech—hyperbole, metaphor, irony, sarcasm—work only if the sender has enough knowledge to know that average house cellars will not hold millions of bottles, women are not made of iron, and so on. When we speak to a child, or to someone from another culture, we can easily estimate this knowledge incorrectly. Children and foreign language learners sometimes take figures of speech literally ('Was Queen Victoria really made of iron, Mummy?', 'You English people must have very big houses'). Through our misjudgement of their knowledge, metaphor becomes a lie, and we are left with the disturbing conclusion that the truth of a message is something constructed by sender and receiver, and not only—as is usually held to be the case—a quality of the sender's intention or the message itself.

Just as the quality maxim can be flouted for effect, so can the other three. The quantity maxim is violated in both directions: creating prolixity if we say too much and terseness if we are too brief. We often say more than we need, perhaps to mark a sense of occasion, or respect; and we often say less than we need, perhaps to be rude, or blunt, or forthright. Sometimes we deliberately flout the charge to be relevant: to signal embarrassment or a desire to change the subject. Lastly, the maxim of manner is violated either for humour, as in the case of puns and *doubles entendres*, where rival meanings are deliberately tolerated, or in order to establish solidarity between speakers and exclude an overhearer from the conversation. Lawyers and judges talk to each other in ways the prisoner in the dock cannot always understand; doctors diagnose patients for medical students in a language which they know the patient will not follow (though there are also valid scientific reasons for this); and parents spell out words they do not want children to understand.

▶ TASK 16

Which maxims of the co-operative principle are being flouted in the following, and why?

1 I think I'll go for a W–A–L–K. (spelling the word letter by letter in front of a dog)

2 Is there anywhere I can powder my nose? (meaning: 'I need a toilet')

3 – I can jump higher than the Empire State Building.
   – Can you?
   – Yes, because buildings can't jump at all. (children's joke)

4 This meal is delicious. (said by a guest who finds the food disgusting)

5 – Then she did a P.G.C.E. in T.E.S.O.L. as they call T.E.F.L. nowadays.
   – Sorry, I don't know what you're talking about.

6 Child: I'm going to watch *Match of the Day* now.
   Parent: What was that Maths homework you said you had?

The meanings created by these floutings, it will be noticed, are often social, signalling the attitude of the sender to the receiver of the message, and the kind of relationship which exists or is developing between them. Grice viewed these attitudinal meanings as being created by departures from the co-operative principle. An alternative way of looking at this is to posit another principle also universally present in human intercourse.

3.9 Conversational principles: politeness

The politeness principle, like the co-operative principle, may be formulated as a series of maxims which people assume are being followed in the utterances of others. As with the co-operative principle any flouting of these maxims will take on meaning, provided it is perceived for what it is. The linguist Robin Lakoff (1973) has formulated these maxims as follows:

– Don't impose
– Give options
– Make your receiver feel good

These maxims of the politeness principle explain many of those frequent utterances in which no new information is communicated. My neighbour said 'I'm sorry. I saw you were home' in an attempt to mitigate the imposition she was making. In English we often give orders, and make requests and pleas (directives) in the form of elaborate questions ('Would you mind . . . Could you possibly . . . May I ask you to . . . ') which give the option of refusal; we apologize for imposing ('I'm sorry to bother you'), and add in praise to make our hearer feel good ('You know much more about car engines than I do'). Clearly the politeness principle and the co-operative principle are often in conflict with each other. Politeness and truth are often mutually incompatible (how do we answer the friend who asks whether we like his new hairstyle, for example?) and so are politeness and brevity. These conflicting demands of the two principles are something of which people are consciously aware. In English, there is even a term for the surrender of truth to politeness: 'a white lie'.

► TASK 17

Here are transcripts of two actual conversations. Can you identify which maxims of co-operation and politeness are being obeyed or flouted?

1   A new teacher has gone to his headteacher's office. The head-teacher is extremely busy preparing for a meeting. The young teacher speaks first.

   A: excuse me are you busy
   B: no not at all
   A: I wondered if I could have a word with you

2   A telephone call. The convention * indicates a substantial pause; # the beginning and end of overlapping speech.

   A: hello Mr Parkin this is Guy Cook here
   B: yes
   A: er do you remember um sending us a er an estimate for electrical repairs * for a hundred and fifty pounds * well I've er just had a word with the Electricity Board with an engineer called Mr Golding and he tells me that the er the list of jobs you gave us unless there's any special circumstances should not be more than around one hundred pounds *
   B: oh *
   A: well he said he'd have to look at it of course but er is there some special reason why you thought it would cost more
   B: no *

A: well would you be prepared to do it for the price he quoted
B: no
A: well why not
B: I can't afford it not with my wages and overheads # I have
A: well # why should I pay an extra fifty pounds if I can get it done cheaper *
B: well if you can do that * do

3.10 The social basis of conversational principles

The co-operative and politeness principles, and the tension between them, reflect a dual purpose in human intercourse: to act efficiently together with other people, and to create and maintain social relationships. There are situations, and there are types of relationships, in which one of these purposes becomes dominant, and the other hardly matters at all. In emergencies, when there is a need for immediate action, it is hardly appropriate to follow the politeness principle. In a cinema, for example, although you would no doubt forgive me if I shouted 'Move!' at you if I had seen that a heavy chandelier was falling on to your head, you might not be so tolerant if I used the same formulation, requesting the same action, if you were simply obscuring my view of the screen. In the latter case I would be more likely to give you options and a reason, by saying: 'Would you mind moving slightly. I can't see the screen very clearly.'

Brown and Levinson (1978), who have studied politeness phenomena in widely diverse languages and cultures, suggest that their origin is the same in all societies. All human beings, in order to enter into social relationships with each other, must acknowledge the *face* of other people. By this they mean that people both avoid intruding upon each other's territory (physical territory, a particular field of knowledge, a friendship) and also seek to enlarge the territory of others—in Lakoff's terms, make the other person feel good—presumably on the assumption that the same will be done to them. The specific nature of face varies from society to society. In some societies, parents have more rights to interfere in the domestic affairs of adult children, for example, than in others. In some cultures, a bedroom is private and cannot be entered without permission, while in others it can. Such differences cause notorious misunderstandings between people from different cultures, who are usually—but not always—speakers of different languages. Moreover, the precise way of indicating respect for face may be culture specific, and not subject to direct translation. In some cultures, initial refusal of an offer may be merely polite, and invite repetition; in others the opposite may be true. Clearly, such issues are vitally important in the teaching and learning of foreign languages. Brown and Levinson's notion of a universal cause behind conversational principles may help both teachers and learners to approach this difficult problem more successfully. Though their realizations differ, the two, often conflicting, aims of communication—to co-operate and to maintain social relations—are universal. The theory also goes some way towards answering the question of why people speak indirectly. It enables them to give options and also to retreat behind the literal meaning of what is said.

3.11 Speech acts

Inferring the function of what is said by considering its form and context is an ability which is essential for the creation and reception of coherent discourse and thus for successful communication. The principles of politeness and co-operation are not, on their own, enough to provide the explanation for this inference. To do this—as we have seen—we also need knowledge of the physical and social world. We also need to make assumptions about the knowledge of the people with whom we are interacting.

An approach which tries to formulate how such knowledge is brought into play is *speech act theory*. This was first formulated by the philosopher John Austin in a series of lectures which are now collected into a short book with the deceptively simple title of *How to do Things with Words* (Austin 1962). These ideas were further developed by another philosopher, John Searle (1969, 1975), who both added to them and presented them more systematically. They have subsequently been developed by other thinkers, but for clarity's sake we shall treat them as a single body of thought.

3.12 Declarations and performatives

Speech act theory begins with the observation that there is a class of highly ritualistic utterances which carry no information about the world outside language at all, because they refer only to themselves. Examples of such utterances are swearing an oath, sentencing a criminal, opening a building, arresting a felon, naming a ship. They are utterances in which saying the words and doing the action are the same thing: the function is created by the form. Such utterances are labelled *declarations*. The utterance 'I sentence you to death' performs the function of sentencing someone to death, and this function is only performed (within certain legal systems) by this utterance. However, the utterance only succeeds in having this function if certain external conditions are fulfilled. The words must be uttered by someone with the necessary authority, in a country in which there is a death penalty, to a person who has been convicted of a particular crime; they must be spoken, not written, at the right time (at the end of a trial) and in the right place (in court). For the words to function as a death sentence, all these conditions must be fulfilled. The judge cannot say them to a member of the family over breakfast, or in a country where the death penalty has been abolished. It is no good my standing up in court and saying them, even to the right person at the right time, because I am not a judge. It is no good the judge's writing the criminal a note; the words must be said out loud. The conditions which must be fulfilled are known as *felicity conditions*.

▶   TASK 18

What are the felicity conditions for the following utterances to function?

1 I pronounce that they be Man and Wife.
2 I name this ship *Aurora*.
3 You are under arrest.
4 I absolve you from all your sins.
5 I declare the said person duly elected to Parliament.

To what extent do such conditions vary from culture to culture?

In most lives, such highly ritualistic utterances as declarations are rare and very dramatic. We may swear an oath only two or three times, and unless we are a judge, or a princess, we are unlikely to sentence anyone or name any ships. The whole issue may seem very far removed from the analysis of discourse and the concerns of the typical language learner. Declarations, however, are only a special case of a much commoner group of utterances, *performatives*. These are also utterances in which saying is doing, and they too are only successful if certain felicity conditions are fulfilled, but, unlike declarations, their related verbs (vow, arrest, declare, etc.) are not always actually said. A good example is the act of ordering someone to do something. To do this it is possible to use the verb 'order' and say, for example, 'I order you to clean your boots', or to use the imperative form 'Clean your boots', which is often associated with ordering. Yet, as with declarations, such utterances will only be perceived as orders if certain conditions are in operation and known to be in operation by both the sender and the receiver. The felicity conditions for an order are:

1 The sender believes the action should be done.
2 The receiver has the ability to do the action.
3 The receiver has the obligation to do the action.
4 The sender has the right to tell the receiver to do the action.

If any one of these conditions is not fulfilled, the utterance will not function as an order. If I order someone to clean their boots when I do not really believe that this should be done, then my order is insincere, and flawed (condition 1). I can order someone to clean their boots, but not to eat the Eiffel Tower—they will not have the ability (condition 2). My order will not succeed as an order unless the person I am talking to is obliged to clean their boots (condition 3), and I have the right and the power to make them do so (condition 4). I could not order you to clean your boots, for example; though I might recommend it. Conversely, we can see that if the conditions do hold, then any reference by the sender to the action will be perceived as an order, even without an explicit form like 'I order you to . . .' or the imperative. Let us imagine a very clear-cut situation in which the power of the sender over the receiver is considerable: an army sergeant speaking to a private just before parade. If this sergeant relates the action of cleaning boots to any of the felicity conditions for orders, if he bellows (or even gently whispers) any of the following:

I think your boots need cleaning, Jones! (condition 1)
I'm bloody sure you can get your boots cleaner than that, Jones! (condition 2)
You're supposed to come on to parade with clean boots, Jones! (condition 3)
It's my job to see you've got cleaner boots than this! (condition 4)

then we may be sure both that the sergeant means his words to be perceived as an order, and that the private will perceive them as such. The private, for his part, may try to challenge the felicity condition invoked, and, if he succeeds, he will take away the status of 'order' from the utterance. He might say

Don't you think having a well-oiled rifle is more important? Or,
I've been scrubbing all morning and they won't come any cleaner. Or,
I didn't see that in the standing orders, sergeant. Or,
The Captain told me it was all right.

In armies the power relations are so clear, and the rights and obligations of the participants so firmly established, that any one of these comments is likely to be punished as facetiousness or disobedience—even though no explicit order has been given. Having exhausted all these possibilities, the ordering and challenging might become explicit.

S:　Jones. Clean your boots.
Pr:　No, sergeant.
S:　Jones, I order you to clean your boots.
Pr:　No, sergeant.
S:　Right, you've had it now. Trying to undermine my authority! You're on a charge!

Speech act theory, which relates the function of utterances to sets of felicity conditions and the knowledge of participants that these conditions exist, may help us to understand the unity of exchanges in communication.

► TASK 19

We have seen how a conversation between a sergeant and a private might proceed by reference to each of the felicity conditions for an order and a challenge to each of them in turn, before becoming more explicit with the use of a direct order and an outright refusal. Imagine a situation in which a teacher is telling a pupil to write a longer answer. Invent a conversation which follows the same stages as that between the sergeant and the private. The original invented exchange is written out on the left. Match each utterance with one on the right.

Sergeant and Private		Teacher and Pupil
S: I think your boots need cleaning, Jones!	(*condition 1*)	T: I think this answer could be a bit longer.
Pr: Don't you think having a well-oiled rifle is more important?	(*challenge*)	Pu: . . . . .
S: I'm bloody sure you can get your boots cleaner than that, Jones!	(*condition 2*)	T: . . . . .
Pr: I've been scrubbing all morning and they won't come any cleaner.	(*challenge*)	Pu: . . . . .
S: You're supposed to come on to parade with clean boots, Jones!	(*condition 3*)	T: . . . . .
Pr: I didn't see that in the standing orders!	(*challenge*)	Pu: . . . . .
S: It's my job to see you've got cleaner boots than this!	(*condition 4*)	T: . . . . .
Pr: The Captain told me it was all right.	(*challenge*)	Pu: . . . . .
S: Jones. Clean your boots!	(*imperative*)	T: . . . . .
Pr: No, sergeant.	(*refusal*)	Pu: . . . . .
S: Jones, I order you to clean your boots.	(*explicit performative*)	T: . . . . .
Pr: No, sergeant.	(*refusal*)	Pu: . . . . .
S: Right, you've had it now. Trying to undermine my authority! You're on a charge!		

3.13 Speech act theory and coherence

Speech act theory provides us with a means of probing beneath the surface of discourse and establishing the function of what is being said. This in turn may help us to postulate structures beneath the surface, sequences and relations of acts, which may help us to go further towards finding the answer to our original problem: what is it that makes stretches of language coherent and communicative? We are moving towards a position in which we shall be able to examine the structure of discourse both in terms of surface relations of form, and underlying relations of functions and acts.

▶ TASK 20

Developing the idea that speech acts can be defined by their felicity conditions, and building upon those for 'orders', we can see that acts form 'families', sharing some conditions and differing in others. The family to which the act of ordering belongs is called *directives*, because they have a directive function. Here is a list of felicity conditions, the first four of which are those for the act of ordering. In the chart which follows the list, distinguish each directive act by ticking the felicity conditions which apply to it.

 1 The sender believes the action should be done.
 2 The receiver has the ability to do the action.
 3 The receiver has the obligation to do the action.
 4 The sender has the right to tell the receiver to do the action.
 5 The sender refers to an action necessary for a particular goal.
 6 The sender refers to an action necessary if the receiver is to avoid unpleasant consequences.
 7 The sender refers to an action which will benefit the receiver.
 8 The sender refers to an action which will benefit the sender.
 9 The sender possesses knowledge which the receiver lacks.
10 The sender cannot carry out the action referred to.

Act	Condition									
	1	2	3	4	5	6	7	8	9	10
Order	✓	✓	✓	✓						
Advise										
Appeal										
Pray										
Warn										

 1 Are these felicity conditions the right ones to distinguish these acts?
 2 Another family of speech acts which has been suggested is *expressives*, which includes the acts of thanking, apologizing, welcoming, and congratulating. Try to list the felicity conditions for each of these acts.
 3 Do the same for the *commissive* acts of promising and threatening.

3.14 Underlying force

Speech act theory uses technical terms for these layers of intention and interpretation. The formal literal meaning of the words is the *locution*; the act which is performed by saying it the *illocution*; a third layer is the *perlocution* or overall aim of the discourse. An utterance is said to have *illocutionary force* and *perlocutionary force*. If we go back to the private's utterance 'I've been scrubbing them all morning and they won't come any cleaner', we can relate it to these three layers as follows:

1 *The locution:* a statement conveying information that the speaker has been cleaning his boots all morning

2 *The illocution:* to challenge the sergeant's order

3 *The perlocution:* to undermine the sergeant's authority, or to be cheeky, or to escape the duty of cleaning the boots.

Notice how meaning becomes more and more slippery as we move from one layer to the next. This is something which human beings exploit to their advantage. It enables them to avoid committing themselves and to retreat in front of danger; and this is one of the major reasons why people speak indirectly. Accused of being insolent, the private may say: 'No I wasn't, sergeant, I was just saying I'd been cleaning my boots.' Indirection also enables us to give others the option of retreat. 'Are you busy?' (Task 16) is a more avoidable request than 'Sit down and talk to me'. Quite often, people explicitly discuss, or try to clarify the illocutionary and perlocutionary force, to formulate the *upshot* of what is said. This is often a major concern of law, where we might hear claims such as:

I suggest that when you told my client he might get hurt you were in fact threatening him. And I suggest that you made a number of such threats which constituted a sustained campaign of intimidation.

Even in more casual situations people often try to get at the upshot of what is being said with such utterances as 'What are you trying to tell me?'

▶ TASK 21

Is upshot confined to words? Consider this (true) example. A court in Oxford heard a case concerning a fight in a Chinese take-away. A man picked up a bottle of soy sauce on his way out, without paying for it. The owner picked up a metal rolling pin, whereupon the man took off his metal studded belt. The jury were asked to decide whether either or both of these actions could be interpreted as a threat. Could speech act theory have helped them decide?

The upshot of non-verbal actions is not always so easily formulated. Sperber and Wilson (1986:55) give two contrasting examples concerning the meaning of a sniff. In one case, a couple return home to a house in which there is a smell of gas. In this case the illocution of the sniff may easily be formulated as 'I can smell gas! Can you?' But suppose the same couple are on holiday by the seaside. On the first morning one of them gets up, goes to the window, draws the curtain, and sniffs ostentatiously. Can we formulate the meaning of this so easily? Are there meanings which do not yield to words?

▶ TASK 22

Look again at the conversations in Task 17. Can you identify the illocutions underlying each utterance? How would you describe the perlocutionary meaning of the two participants? What is the illocutionary force of the sergeant's last utterance in Task 19? How does he interpret the upshot of the private's words?

Now look at the following transcripts of exchanges between a husband and wife. How does **A** exploit ambiguity in the illocutionary force of what is said? Identify utterances which try to formulate explicitly the upshot of what is being said. Do these utterances refer to the illocutionary or the perlocutionary force?

Exchange 1
A: Are you planning to do it this afternoon?
B: *(angrily)* Well WHEN this afternoon?
A: *(with injured innocence)* I'm just asking whether you'll be able to do it this afternoon.

Exchange 2
B: Oh no we haven't got the TV programme.
A: Go and get one then.
B: Go and get one! I've just come in.
A: Well if you don't go I'll go.
B: That's blackmail.
A: It's not blackmail, it's just a FACT.

3.15 Pragmatics, discourse analysis, and language teaching

In 3 we have discussed theories of the pragmatic interpretation of language: how people create meaning and make sense of what is said in specific circumstances. The fact that meaning is not constructed from the formal language of the message alone is crucial in explaining what it is that makes people perceive some stretches of language as coherent discourse and others as disconnected jumbles. It is also important for the successful teaching and learning of foreign languages.

The importance of pragmatic theories in language learning is really twofold. Firstly, the divergence of function and form means that we cannot rely upon teaching only form. In production, learners need to choose the words which most suitably realize their intention, and this does not always entail the most closely related form; in reception of language, given the human penchant for indirection, they also need to be able to move from the form to the function. There are times when making language function effectively is more important than producing perfectly pronounced, grammatically correct sentences.

Secondly, the linking of form to function may help learners to orientate themselves within a discourse. All learners of a foreign language are familiar with the disturbing sensation of understanding every word, and the literal meaning, but somehow missing the point. The underlying structure of the discourse may be a progression of functional units, and a breakdown in pragmatic interpretation may easily lead to a learner losing his or her way. We shall need to go further in examining how functional units interact to create discourse, and how the learner may be guided through them. We shall return to this in Section Two.

These two points raise the issue of the extent to which pragmatic interpretation and discourse structure are culture specific, and the extent to which they need to be—or can be—taught. In order to 'do things with words' either actively, as language producers, or passively, as language understanders, we clearly need more tools than the formal language system, though we do need that too. The needs of the language user might be represented as in Figure 2.

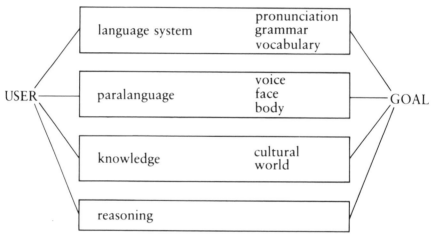

Figure 2

Traditionally, language teaching has concentrated only on the three levels of the formal language system—pronunciation, grammar, and vocabulary—and the way in which they function within the sentence, on the assumption that other aspects of communication will follow fairly automatically. It remains true, of course, that the formal system of a foreign language is very obviously different from that of the learner's first language, that it therefore forms the basis of any full communication, and that it needs to be acquired in some way. It is not, however, all that is needed for communication. So far, in our search for the forces which create coherence, we have examined some of the other factors in communication. In 2 we have looked at how the formal system operates between as well as within sentences; in 3 we have seen how knowledge of the world (about cats and gates, for example) or of the culture (about social roles and relationships) enables people to make their language function as they intend and to understand how others do the same to them. To connect their knowledge with the language system people use reasoning, and pragmatic theories go some way towards explaining how people reason their way from the form to the function and thus construct coherent discourse from the language they receive. There is still a great deal to say about this interaction of knowledge, reasoning, and language, and we shall be exploring it further in **4** to **6**.

What we need to decide as language teachers is the degree to which other components of communication need teaching. All human beings have reasoning power, world knowledge, and knowledge of at least one culture; but the divisions between these categories, and the nature of their contents are not always clear. How far do conversational principles and the interpretation of speech acts proceed differently in different cultures, for example? We also need to help learners integrate the components of communication one with another. It is no good teaching them as discrete units and hoping that the learner, suddenly faced with a communicative situation, will be able to integrate them all with immediate success. Whatever cultural variation there may be in pragmatic interpretation, we may be sure that its interaction with form is language specific. It does need teaching, though we must be careful not to go to the opposite extreme, as many courses do, and patronizingly treat adult learners like new-born babes. They bring with them immense reasoning power, knowledge of the world, and a sophisticated skill at implementing through their own language and culture the complex needs of all humans; to relate to others, and to act with them.

The pragmatic theories we have examined leave a number of unanswered questions, and they are in need of considerable extension before they can be fruitfully applied to discourse analysis and language teaching. It is not always clear, for example, where the context of an utterance ends (Cook 1986b), and even when that is established we are still left with the vagueness of the central concept of relevance. How do human beings distinguish which of the many elements of the context are relevant? We shall return to this later. Another weakness is the implicit assumption that underlying meaning can always be formulated in words. Speech act theory assumes that there is one neat, verbally expressible illocution to each locution.

The theories of pragmatic language use are from philosophy rather than linguistics, and the examples used are invented and stylized. They concern spoken discourse in which sender and receiver interact with each other rapidly, and they tend to be short and deal with a few turns at most. This is not a criticism of the theories in themselves, but if discourse analysis is to incorporate them, and to demonstrate their relevance to the language learner, it will need to test their value in interpreting language which has actually occurred; to select what is relevant from context rather than invent a few elements of it; to account for writing as well as speech, and to account for discourse where there is no constant feedback from the receiver—who may not even be present. And it will need to deal with long stretches of language, rather than handfuls of utterances. We shall next examine ways in which this might be done.

4 Two views of discourse structure: as product and as process

4.1 Introduction

Pragmatics provides us with a means of relating stretches of language to the physical, social, and psychological world in which they take place. Discourse, indeed, might be defined as the totality of all these elements interacting. Yet pragmatics tends only to examine how meaning develops at a given point. It provides us with something like a snapshot of meaning. Discourse is more like a moving film, revealing itself in time—sometimes over long periods.

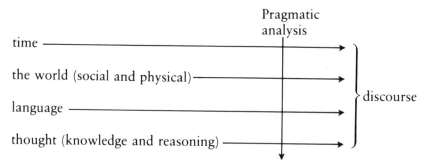

Figure 3

Foreign language learners need to enter into long stretches of communication, in real and complex situations. We need to build further on the ideas we have covered so far, to look at longer stretches of discourse, to form a picture of discourses in totalities rather than in extracts.

4.2 Rank structure

One way of representing the relationship of parts to a whole is as a *rank structure*, in which each rank is made up of one or more of the rank below. This type of analysis is used in linguistics, to describe the grammar of sentences. The ranks of grammar are
- Sentence
- Clause
- Phrase
- Word

and the structure of a particular sentence can be represented as in Figure 4.

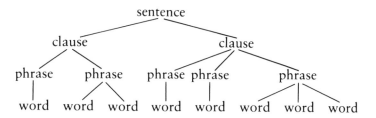

Figure 4

This is known as a *tree diagram* (although it looks more like roots than branches). As each element may consist of *one or more* of the elements of the line below, it is possible for a sentence to consist of a single clause which consists of a single phrase which consists of a single word. 'Go!', for example, is at once a sentence, a clause, a phrase, and a word.

The idea of rank structure and its representation in tree diagrams can be borrowed from grammar and applied to discourse. If we regard a three-volume series of books as a complete discourse, for example, we can render its structure as in Figure 5.

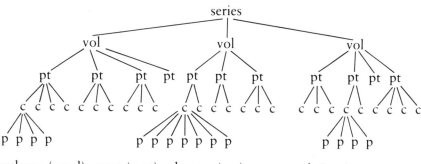

volume (=vol)   part (=pt)   chapter (=c)   paragraph (=p)

Figure 5

Notice that what is proposed here is not a rank structure applicable to all discourse in the way that the grammatical rank structure is applicable to all sentences, but a structure specific to a particular discourse type.

▶ TASK 23

In many countries, a criminal trial has the following stages: indictment, prosecution case, defence case, summing up, verdict, sentence. The defence and prosecution cases are each made up of an introduction, testimonies of witnesses, and a summary. Each testimony consists of examination and cross-examination, and each of these consists of questions and answers.

– Draw up ranks and a typical tree diagram for the discourse type:
trial.
– How much do you think the structure of discourse types varies
between cultures?

4.3 The Birmingham School of Discourse Analysis

In the discourse types explored above the boundaries of units are clearly
marked. Volumes are physically separate; parts and chapters are labelled as
such; paragraphs are marked off by indentation and are visible without
reading the words. Similarly the stages of a formal spoken discourse are
also often clearly marked with utterances such as 'I rest my case', 'Let me
ask you another question', or 'Next witness'. Other discourse types do not
have such overtly marked units; but they may also be susceptible to the
same representation.

A pioneering and influential study in this field was carried out at the
University of Birmingham by Sinclair and Coulthard (1975). To teachers, it
is of particular interest not only because it provides a model which might be
applied with modifications to discourse in general, but also because the
discourse type it chose to analyse was school lessons.

Sinclair and Coulthard recorded a number of British primary school
lessons. On the basis of these data they proposed a rank structure for these
lessons as follows:
– Lesson
– Transaction
– Exchange
– Move
– Act
Acts, the lowest rank in this scale, are speech acts of the kind discussed in **3**.
From their data, Sinclair and Coulthard identified a finite number used by
the teachers and pupils and gave each one a code as in Table 1.

Code	Act	Function	Realisation (e.g.)
acc	Accept	Shows T has heard correct information	'Yes', 'Good', 'Fine'
ack	Acknowledge	Shows P has understood, intends to react	'Yes', 'OK', 'mmhm', 'Wow'
z	Aside	T talking to himself/herself	Statement/question/command
b	Bid	Signals desire to contribute	'Miss!' 'Sir!' Raised hand
ch	Check	Checks progress	'Finished?' 'Ready?' Questions
c	Cue	Evokes bid	'Hands up!' 'Don't call out!'
cl	Clue	Gives extra information	Statement/question/command
com	Comment	Exemplifies/expands/justifies	Statement/tag question
con	Conclusion	Summarises	'So, what we've been doing is . . .'
d	Directive	Requests action	Imperative
el	Elicitation	Requests answer	Question
e	Evaluation	Evaluates	'Good', 'Interesting', 'Yes'
i	Information	Provides information	Statement
l	Loop	Returns to point before P's answer	'Pardon?', 'Again?'
m	Marker	Marks boundary in discourse	'Well', 'OK', 'Right'
ms	Metastatement	Explicitly refers to development of lesson	Statement
n	Nomination	Tells or permits a P to contribute	'You', 'Yes', 'Jane'
p	Prompt	Reinforces directive or elicitation	'Go on', 'Hurry up'
rea	React	Provides appropriate reply to directive	Non-linguistic
rep	Reply	Provides appropriate reply to elicitation	Statement/question/nod
^	Silent Stress	Highlights marker	Pause
s	Starter	Provides information to facilitate response	Statement/question/command

Key
T = teacher
P = pupil

Table 1 (*based on Sinclair and Coulthard 1975:40–44*)

They then drew up rules, based on the data, showing how these acts combine together to form moves and how moves combine to form various kinds of exchange—rather as grammarians formulate rules describing how words combine into phrases, or phrases into clauses. One kind of exchange, which they called a teaching exchange, for example, consisted of between one and three moves:

Opening   (Answering)   (Follow-up)

(An element within brackets here and in Figure 6 is optional.) Going down to the next layer, each of these moves consists of specified acts, as in Figure 6.

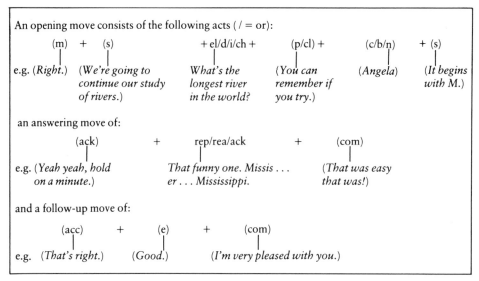

Figure 6 (*Invented example based on Sinclair and Coulthard 1975*)

▶ TASK 24

Here is a transcript of part of an English lesson in a British secondary school (for conventions, see Task 17). Try to code the acts according to the Sinclair and Coulthard system and show how they combine into moves and exchanges. What problems do you encounter?

T: two things to establish for the writer at the beginning of the story one the situation what is the situation * at the beginning of the story * anybody what's the situation Douglas * have you read the story Douglas

S: no sir

T: ah that won't help then will it who's read the story what is the situation at the beginning * Michael * is it Michael

SS: (*laughter*)

T: # is it Michael

S: Carl #

T: what's the situation at the beginning simple detail situation what where what is the story about at the beginning * have you read it

S: no sir

T: right who's read it * Sarah

(*Walsh 1987:82*)

The Birmingham School approach has since been applied to many different discourse types: for example, medical consultations (Coulthard and Montgomery 1981b) and TV quiz shows (Berry 1981). The importance of such approaches for the language learner is that if people involved in communication know, even subconsciously, of the structures of various discourse types and the way they develop, then this tacit knowledge may enable them to communicate successfully. The primary school pupils studied by Sinclair and Coulthard had acquired such a knowledge of the way lessons develop; the participants in a trial know what stage it is in and can organize their behaviour accordingly. Because such structures are 'conventional, and hence culturally variable' (van Dijk and Kintsch 1983:16) the language learner, in order to be able to operate effectively as a participant in discourse, needs to be able both to identify what type of discourse he or she is involved in, and to predict how it will typically be structured. Again, this may explain that phenomenon which is central to the relevance of discourse analysis to language teaching: how is it that a student with an advanced proficiency in pronunciation, grammar, and lexis somehow fails to use these language skills to communicate successfully?

▶ TASK 25

Here are two more extracts from secondary English classes. What problems do they present for the Sinclair and Coulthard coding system and how could it be adjusted to cope with them?

Extract 1
T: You're a big bully Denise.
S1: No I ain't am I Sharon?
S2: No she ain't. She's nice.

Extract 2
T: Answer the question will you?
S1: Oh leave us alone for a second, we're just discussin' somethin'.
S2: Somethin' interestin'.
(*Cook 1987:56*)

The discourse types to which this approach is most easily applied tend to have certain features in common. They are all rather formal and ritualistic, and feature one participant with the institutionalized power to direct the discourse. This person may well plan the development of the discourse in advance (as is hopefully the case with lessons) within the fairly narrow limits of the social conventions for that discourse type. There are cases where participants depart from the plans and conventions, of course. This is sometimes interpreted as insubordination, crime, madness, immaturity, or ignorance; sometimes as a sign that the speaker is foreign—and sometimes as creativity!

4.4 Discourse typology: spoken and written; formal and informal

The Birmingham School approach examines spoken discourse, seeking to interpret it in terms of a rank structure and showing that when it is analysed after the event, there is more order and form in it than might at first be apparent. We need now to assess the validity of this approach, to see whether it can be extended to other kinds of discourse, and to examine alternative approaches too. As a preliminary we shall begin to examine the problem of how different kinds of discourse can be categorized, and the parameters which are best used to distinguish them.

Traditionally, language teaching has divided discourse into two major categories, the spoken and the written, further divided into the four skills of speaking and listening, writing and reading. Many courses try to provide a balanced coverage. Spoken discourse is often considered to be less planned and orderly, more open to intervention by the receiver. There are some kinds of spoken discourse, however—like lessons, lectures, interviews, and trials—which have significant features in common with typical written discourse. As we have seen in our summary of the Birmingham School approach, these kinds of spoken discourse are also planned, and the possibilities for subordinate participants can be severely limited. It is clear that in reading a novel one cannot influence its development (that can be the pleasure or pain of reading), but it is almost equally hard for a criminal to influence the direction of a trial, or for a primary school pupil to prevent the lesson progressing as the teacher intends. Conversely, there are times when readers do have rights to affect written discourse. Writers respond to the market. Teachers send essays back to be rewritten. The editors of this book may ask me to cut out this sentence.

The traditional division of language into the spoken and the written is clearly and sensibly based on a difference in production and reception: we use our mouths and ears for one, and our hands and eyes for the other. Yet as far as discourse structure is concerned, a more fundamental distinction seems to be between formal, planned discourse, which may be either written or spoken, and less formal, unplanned discourse which—though it may also be either written or spoken—is usually associated with speech. Informal spoken discourse is something in which the modern foreign language learner, with opportunities for travel and social contact, is most likely to wish to succeed, but also the discourse type he or she is likely to find hardest, precisely because it is so informal and unpredictable. It is a common and enormously frustrating experience for foreign language learners, presented with the opportunity to participate in authentic conversation with native speakers, to fail to join in successfully, despite having a high level of proficiency in the classroom. Conversation is fast, and to some extent this failure of the foreign language learner can be attributed to the slow processing of language knowledge. By the time the learner has formulated something to say, the conversation has moved on. Yet there are other reasons too.

4.5 Conversation as a discourse type

The term *conversation* is widely used, in a non-technical sense, and people seem capable of distinguishing it from other kinds of talk. They mean, broadly speaking, that the talk is less formal. Discourse analysts are rather vague about what they mean by 'conversation' too, and some seem to use the term to describe any kind of oral interaction. We shall define the term as follows. Talk may be classed as conversation when:

1 It is not primarily necessitated by a practical task.
2 Any unequal power of participants is partially suspended.
3 The number of participants is small.
4 Turns are quite short.
5 Talk is primarily for the participants and not for an outside audience.

These definitions are imprecise. For example, considering (3), there is no fixed number of participants at which conversation becomes impossible, but although a conversation can take place between five people, it cannot take place between a hundred. Or again, considering (4), there is no fixed length for turns in conversation, and sometimes one participant holds the floor for some time; yet although we might call a turn of four minutes part of a conversation, we would consider conversation to have ceased if someone talked for an hour and a half. Nevertheless, the definitions are useful despite their imprecision.

The boundary between conversation and other discourse types is a fuzzy one, and there are many intermediate cases. A seminar, for example, might come somewhere between the two poles. We can represent the difference between the two as a *cline*, or continuum, with extreme cases at either end and a range of intermediate possibilities in between:

Formal spoken discourse ————————————————————— Conversation

There are many polar opposites in discourse classification, but they are usually best represented in this way, as we shall see later.

Talk at the conversation end of the cline is difficult to mould to any overall structure like that proposed by Sinclair and Coulthard. Indeed it might seem initially that a part of the definition of conversation might be its unpredictability and lack of structure.

▶ TASK 26

    A: Come in Highland Boy. Can you hear me? Over.
    B: Yes I can hear you. What's the weather like up there? Over.

A: Fine. Over.
B: Good. Keep smiling. Over and out.

What are the conventions of radio conversations like this one, and why are they different from those of face-to-face conversation?

4.6 Conversation analysis

Conversation analysis, which is sometimes regarded as distinct from discourse analysis (Levinson 1983:286), is a branch of study which sets out to discover what order there might be in this apparent chaos. It is often associated with a group of scholars in the USA known as *ethnomethodologists*: because they (*—ists*) set out to discover what methods (*—methodolog—*) people (*ethno—*) use to participate in and make sense of interaction.

Rather than try to impose large structures on what is happening from the outset, they begin at the most local level, trying to see how participants in interaction handle conversation: how they judge who can speak, and when. Working on corpora of North American conversational data, they proceed very much from the *bottom-up* trying to establish the smallest units first. Indeed they regard work like that of Sinclair and Coulthard as over-hasty 'premature formalization' (Levinson 1983:287). Rather than wait until a discourse is finished, and then analyse it as a whole, from outside and with the benefit of hindsight, the ethnomethodologists try to understand how it unfolds in time. They view discourse as a developing process, rather than a finished product; and this, after all, is how the participants must be handling it and making sense of it, without the benefit of transcription and *post hoc* theorizing.

4.7 Turn-taking

The ethnomethodologists' starting point is the very basic observation that conversation involves turn-taking and that the end of one speaker's turn and the beginning of the next's frequently latch on to each other with almost perfect precision and split-second timing (Sacks, Schegloff, and Jefferson 1974). Overlap of turns occurs in only about 5 per cent of conversation or less, strongly suggesting that speakers somehow know exactly when and where to enter (Ervin-Tripp 1979). They signal to each other that one turn has come to an end and another should begin. Where there is overlap between turns it has some particular significance: signalling annoyance, urgency, or a desire to correct what is being said. Conversely, pauses between turns also carry particular meaning. Conversation analysis tries to describe how people take turns, and under what circumstances they overlap turns or pause between them.

The significance of this approach for the language learner is considerable. Turn-taking mechanisms, the way in which speakers hold or pass the floor, vary between cultures and between languages. Overlap in a given situation is more or less tolerated in some societies than in others. There are particular signals which enable speakers to get into—and to get out of—conversations, to pass the turn to somebody else, varying according to whom one is talking to and in what circumstances. These mechanisms cannot simply be lifted from one society (and thus from one language via literal translation) to another. This goes a long way towards explaining the awkwardness felt by the foreign learner in conversation—an awkwardness which does not seem wholly attributable to faulty or slow processing of grammar and vocabulary.

Efficient turn-taking also involves factors which are not linguistic. Eye contact is one strong means of signalling, and in British culture (in very general terms) it can often be observed that speakers look away during their turn and then look their interlocutor in the eye at the end. Body position and movement also play an important part—although the fact that turns latch on to each other successfully in telephone conversations seems to suggest that these factors, like gaze, are perhaps not as important as might at first appear. Intonation and volume contribute to turn-taking too.

The relative status of the speakers, or the role which one of them is playing, are also important. In formal situations roles can clearly give people special rights, but even in conversation—where according to our definition unequal power is suspended—it is unlikely that knowledge of participants' social office or status will be wholly forgotten. Students fall silent when the professor speaks—in the bar as well as the seminar.

▶ TASK 27

Listen carefully to a fragment of real conversation, and if possible record it. How do the participants gain and pass turns? Do their turns latch or overlap, or are there pauses between them?

(If you use a broadcast conversation—for example a TV chat show—remember that although it shares many features with private conversation it will also have an important difference: that the participants are speaking for an audience as well as for themselves.)

4.8 Turn types

One kind of turn alternation the ethnomethodologists describe is an *adjacency pair*. This occurs when the utterance of one speaker makes a particular kind of response very likely. A greeting, for example, is likely to be answered by another greeting, a summons by an answer. If they are not, we are likely to interpret this somehow: as rudeness perhaps, or deafness, or lack of attention. In an adjacency pair, there is often a choice of two likely responses. A request is most likely to be followed by either an acceptance or a refusal. In such cases, one of the responses is termed the preferred response (because it occurs most frequently) and the other the *dispreferred response* (because it is less common). Examples of adjacency pairs are shown in Figure 7.

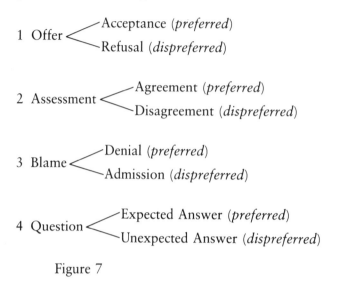

1 Offer — Acceptance (*preferred*) / Refusal (*dispreferred*)

2 Assessment — Agreement (*preferred*) / Disagreement (*dispreferred*)

3 Blame — Denial (*preferred*) / Admission (*dispreferred*)

4 Question — Expected Answer (*preferred*) / Unexpected Answer (*dispreferred*)

Figure 7

A dispreferred response is usually marked in some way: by a slight pause, or by a preface like 'Well' or 'You see', or by an explanation and justification of the response. Sometimes the second part of an adjacency pair can be delayed by an alternation of turns occurring within it. For example:

A: Did you enjoy the meal?
B: (Did you?
A: Yes.)
B: So did I.

in which one question and answer pair contains another, like this: (Q (Q–A) A). This is known as an *insertion sequence*.

The topic of an insertion sequence is intimately related to that of the main sequence in which it occurs. Sometimes, however, speakers simply switch from one topic to another unrelated one, and then back again. In this latter case the insertion is known as a *side sequence*. In the following, for example, the speakers alternate between the main topic of the aerobics and the lesser topic of the missing watch:

A: I'm dying to know—where's my watch by the way?*
B: What?
A: What Gillian's aerobics sessions are like HA HA HA HA
B: What aerobics sessions? It's here.
A: Gillian does aerobics sessions every evening. LEADS them. Thanks. Can you imagine.

Insertion and side sequences draw attention to the fact that conversation is discourse mutually constructed and negotiated in time. Unlike most written discourse and a good deal of spoken discourse like lectures, broadcasts, and speeches, a conversation is constructed and executed as it happens, by two people, feeling their way forward together. There is no going back, crossing out, rewriting and restructuring. This is particularly evident in the phenomenon known as *repair*, in which participants correct either their own words or those of another participant, edging towards a situation in which maximum communication is achieved. In the following extract, for example, one speaker uses a multiply ambiguous term 'child bar' which the other does not understand, causing a temporary breakdown in communication. Together they negotiate a solution to the problem, the first speaker **A** asking the second **B** to repair the term by making it more specific, and the second several times repairing his own explanation to make it clearer (capitals indicate stress):

A: what have you got to do this afternoon
B: oh I'm * going to repair the child bar
A: what do you mean CHILD bar
B: uh it's er metal bar goes acr— has to be fixed from one side of the car I mean from one side of the back seat to the other for the BABY seat to go on
A: AH::::

This kind of mutual formulation of the right amount of information for communication to take place is very common in conversation, particularly where times or places or objects need to be specified. Here is another example:

A: you've got his number haven't you
B: yes I HAVE   .
A: where is it
B: it's in my WALlet on his card
A: where's your wallet
B: in my blue jacket
A: # .hhhh where's
B: in the cupboard #

A further type of clarification is achieved by formulations of the *gist* or the upshot (cf. **3.14**) of what is being said. In the former, the speaker goes back over, or summarizes, the literal (locutionary) meaning of what has been said—and this is typically marked by phrases like 'I'll just go over the main points again'. (This is actually quite formal, and comparatively rare in conversation.) In the case of upshot, it is the illocutionary or perlocutionary force, what the speaker is trying to do with his or her words, which is made explicit, and this may be prefaced by utterances like: 'Are you trying to annoy me?' or 'What's the point of telling me this?' or 'I was only trying to be friendly'. Clearly, formulations of gist and upshot are important in written and formal spoken discourse too, although there the task of the sender is much harder, as he or she has to estimate the need for reformulation at any given point.

Participants in conversation draw attention to, or prepare the ground for, the kind of turn they are going to take next. The utterances which do this are known as *pre-sequences*. They are rather like the markers teachers use to signal transitions in lessons: 'Right!', or 'OK, let's get started!' In conversation, there are many kinds of pre-sequences. The following invented dialogue, for example, begins with a pre-request:

A: Have you got any jazz?
B: Yes.
A: Can I put one on?

And this one with a pre-invitation:

A: Are you free tonight?
B: Yes.
A: Like to go to that film?

Often these act as devices for obtaining the right to a longer turn, like a story. In English, the most obvious examples of this are the clichéd openings of jokes like 'Have you heard the one about the . . . ?' or personal anecdotes: 'Listen! Do you know what happened to us last night?' These also defend the speaker against refusal and save time, by determining whether to continue.

If a right to a longer turn is obtained its ending must also be signalled so that the other participants know it is finished and a contribution from them will not be construed as an interruption. Such signals may include pauses, particular kinds of laughter, and particular filler words like 'Anyway . . .' or 'So . . .'. This brings us to another sequence of turns: the peculiar mechanisms of closing a conversation. In British and North American English this often consists of a pre-sequence which signals impending closure, echoed by the other participant, followed by farewells, like this:

A: I'll ring you Thursday night then
B: all right * ring us Thursday
A: yes I will *
B: bye bye then dear
A: bye

This structure both avoids abrupt closure, which would be construed as rudeness, and gives the option of reopening after the pre-sequence, thus ensuring that neither participant is deprived of the right to add something forgotten.

▶ TASK 28

Identify the turn types and turn-taking mechanisms in the following extracts:

Extract 1

A: so if there's a hardware store we could call in and get one on the way back

B: do you think there is one

A: yes

B: OK then *

A: that would be nice wouldn't it?

B: yes it would

A: I mean the job not the hardware shop

B: yes I REAlize what do you keep telling me for

Extract 2

oh listen I wanted to tell you one of the girls in my supply class we'll hoover when we come back won't we she said to me she looked at my shoes and she said you've got flashy shoes or something I said I got them in Spain she said Miss are you Spanish I thought it was really funny

Record and transcribe an equally short stretch of conversation. Identify the turn types.

4.9 Discourse as process

Ethnomethodology depicts conversation as discourse constructed and negotiated between the participants, following pre-established patterns, and marking the direction they are taking in particular ways: with pauses, laughter, intonations, filler words, and established formulae. These conventions enable the participants to orientate to what is happening, and rapidly make sense of the interaction. For the discourse analyst, it provides another way of accounting for sequences of utterances, though one apparently limited to discourse which is the mutual construction of more than one person. For the language teacher it provides powerful clues concerning the causes of the sensation of floundering in conversation to which we referred earlier. Culture-specific rules and procedures of turn-taking provide ample breeding ground for misunderstanding. Entering and leaving conversation, bidding for a longer turn, refusing without appearing rude, changing the topic, are all notoriously difficult for foreign learners: tasks for which the language classroom, where turns are patiently organized and controlled by the teacher, has hardly prepared them. Indeed the teacher who constantly interrupts the students' discourse to correct every grammatical mistake not only violates usual turn-taking procedures but may also hinder the students' acquisition of them.

▶ TASK 29

Can we or should we attempt to teach turn-taking? What is the source of misunderstanding in the following ending to a conversation between an English native speaker (N) and a foreign learner (F), and how would you remedy it?

N: anyway . . . * well anyway . . . * I'm going * goodbye
F: but you have not finished your sentence
N: what sentence
F: you have said 'anyway . . .'
N: yes
F: anyway * and what

4.10 Conclusion

The two approaches to discourse which we have considered in 4 may seem irreconcilable and applicable to very different kinds of interaction. The Birmingham School has dealt only with formal discourse, and with large structures which become evident after the event; the ethnomethodologists have eschewed these large structures and concerned themselves with local transitions and only with casual conversation. The possibility remains, however, that the two approaches may be developed and reconciled, and a work by Reichman (1985) has achieved some success in compiling exhaustive formulae for the combinations of moves in conversation, and linking these to particular turn-taking mechanisms. Interestingly, the largest structure in this formulation is not the exchange or transaction of the Birmingham School analyses, but a claim by one speaker which gives rise to fixed possibilities for moves of support or counter claim, in patterns referred to as *context spaces*. Movement within and between these context spaces can then be linked to specific turn-taking devices. But both research and theory into the structure and mechanisms of conversation have a very long way to go.

5 Discourse as dialogue

5.1 Introduction

Piecemeal, we are beginning to build up a number of different techniques of analysis which will provide an answer to our initial problem: what is it that gives stretches of language in use their meaning and their unity? We have looked at the devices which create formal links between sentences; at pragmatic interpretations which link literal meaning to function and social meaning; at the existence of hierarchical structures in particular discourse types; and finally at the conversational mechanisms which enable people to construct informal discourse together and make sense of what is happening as they do so.

To the last of these, it might be objected that its relevance is severely limited. Whereas the other approaches seem potentially applicable to discourse in general, conversation analysis, by definition, seems only applicable to discourse of a particular type: spoken, informal interaction. Some of the devices observed by conversation analysts—pausing, overlapping, drawing in breath—are of their nature limited to spoken discourse; yet what they effect, the alternation of one point of view with another, and thus the mutual construction of a discourse, is far more widely applicable. Here we shall argue that dialogue is one of the fundamental structuring principles of all discourse, written and spoken alike. Paradoxically, this is as true in discourse which appears to be created by one person alone (*monologue*) as in discourse which is created by two or more (*dialogue*).

5.2 Dialogue in communicative development

Developmentally, dialogue comes first, both for the human species, and for the human individual. We have no hard evidence of the origins of language in prehistoric communities, but it seems reasonable to assume that speech preceded writing and dialogue preceded monologue. Interestingly, some of the earliest written texts of Western European culture, the Socratic dialogues, present as conversation what modern writers would present as monologue. Perhaps some of this preference remains in modern practices which favour face-to-face interaction: lectures, job interviews, and news interviews.

As with societies, so with each individual infant. Turn-taking and interaction are among the first communicative skills. Parents hold 'conversations', even with very young babies, as the following 'dialogue' between a mother and her two-month-old daughter clearly shows:

M: Whatcha gonna tell me?
B: ⟨*Gurgling noise*⟩
M: Come on whatcha gonna tell me?
B: ⟨*Two gurgling noises. Squeak. Blows air through lips*⟩
M: That's a nice story. What else are you gonna tell me? Come on.
B: ⟨*Gurgling and dribbling noise*⟩
M: Let's hear some more.
(*Baby Talk*—BBC radio programme)

Here the mother is interpreting the child's earliest noises as turns, a phenomenon which has led some researchers to wonder whether the turn-taking mechanisms of conversation, and ability to recognize the kind of turn that is in use, might be the initial framework into which the child gradually fills the details of the language, working *top-down*, from the largest structures to the smallest, as well as—or perhaps instead of—bottom-up, as has usually been assumed.

5.3 Discourse typology: reciprocity

In discourse analysis it has been fairly common to distinguish between two fundamental types of discourse: *reciprocal* and *non-reciprocal*. Discourse is reciprocal when there is at least a potential for interaction, when the sender can monitor reception and adjust to it—or, to put it another way, where the receiver can influence the development of what is being said. In non-reciprocal discourse, sender and receiver may have no opportunity for interaction. The prototype of reciprocal discourse is face-to-face conversation. The prototype of non-reciprocal discourse is a book by a dead author. The distinction, however, is misleading.

Using a cline we can place reciprocal and non-reciprocal discourse at opposite poles:

Reciprocal ——————————————————————— Non-reciprocal

If we assign positions to particular instances of discourse we find firstly that there are many intermediate cases, and secondly that absolutely non-reciprocal discourse is unlikely. Even writers working in solitude try to form some idea of the receiver of their work and adjust to it—the meaningfulness of what they say can be viewed as a measure of the success of that prediction and adjustment. People on television often behave as though they are interacting with us; they look at the camera and address themselves to us, and though this seems to be a fiction, because we cannot interrupt or contradict, still we can switch off or over, and TV programmes are influenced by viewers' letters and ratings.

▶ TASK 30

Where would you place the following on the cline of reciprocal–non-reciprocal discourse?

1 a TV news broadcast
2 a church service
3 a message beamed into outer space in search of intelligent life
4 a letter
5 testimony in court
6 a TV phone-in
7 *Hamlet*
8 an inaugural address by a Head of State
9 a chat with your next door neighbour
10 a lecture

What problems arise in placing these instances on the cline? Add in some more examples of your own.

It should be clear from Task 30 that reciprocity is a question of degree. All discourse is more or less reciprocal, if only because it is based upon assumptions about receivers. It should also be clear that although there is a general tendency for speech to be more reciprocal and writing to be less so, this is by no means necessarily true, and the reciprocal–non-reciprocal cline, like the formal–informal cline, cuts across the distinction between speech and writing. A monarch's speech at a state opening of parliament, though spoken, is far from the reciprocal end of the scale, but a scribbled memo from one teacher to another, though written, may trigger off a series of replies and counter replies, and is thus highly reciprocal.

5.4 Reciprocity, dialogue, and word order

So far we have been talking about the reciprocity of all discourse in the broadest of terms, connecting it to the mechanisms of dialogue only generally by saying that monologues are often constructed with the receiver in mind. Yet this structuring of discourse along the patterns of dialogue has an effect at the most detailed, grammatical level.

In 2 we looked at the details of formal lexical and grammatical connections between sentences in monologue. Another kind of formal connection in monologic discourse is very intimately related to dialogue with an imagined receiver. We might even be justified as regarding the end of each sentence as the point at which the sender assesses the effect on a potential receiver, imagines a reply, and adjusts the next sentence accordingly.

If we want to tell somebody a fact about the world—let's say that John ate fish and chips—we have a number of ways in which we can put this into a sentence. We could say simply

– John ate fish and chips

but there are many other ways of saying the same thing:

- It was John who ate fish and chips.
- What John did was eat fish and chips.
- The person who ate fish and chips was John.
- Fish and chips were eaten by John.
- Eating fish and chips is what John did.
- Fish and chips John ate.
- Fish is what John ate—and chips.

Some of these seem very strange, and many people feel, when first confronted with examples like the last three, that they are odd, unlikely, or just downright wrong. But actual discourse provides a surprising number. Odd they may seem, but occur they do! Like this one!

▶ TASK 31

Without adding or subtracting information, how many ways can you find of rephrasing this sentence?

From the beginning of next month, most of the major banks in Britain will issue cheque cards featuring a colour hologram of William Shakespeare.
(*New Scientist*, 8 September 1988)

The strange thing about these different ways of arranging the same information is that they all apparently mean exactly the same thing. The information in all the versions is the same—no more and no less. Could it be that we just select randomly, in free variation, perhaps to add a little variety for its own sake?

▶ TASK 32

The following are both sequences of grammatically correct sentences. They both contain exactly the same information. One of them is the beginning of the biographical sketch of Ernest Hemingway as it appears in the Penguin edition of his novel *For Whom the Bell Tolls*; the other is the same biographical sketch with the order of information in each sentence altered. Can you tell which is which? If you can, how did you do it?

Version 1
It was in 1899 that Ernest Miller Hemingway was born in Oak Park, a highly respectable suburb of Chicago. Being a doctor was the occupation of his father, a keen sportsman. Of six children, Ernest was the second. A lakeside hunting lodge in Michigan, near Indian settlements, was the place where holidays were spent by the family. Although in school activities Ernest was energetic and successful,

twice he ran away from home before the *Kansas City Star* was joined by him as a cub reporter in 1917. The Italian front was the place where he volunteered to be an ambulance driver during the next year, and was badly wounded. Writing features for the *Toronto Star Weekly* was what he did when he returned to America in 1919. 1921 was the year he married. As a roving correspondent he came to Europe that year, and several large conferences were covered by him.

Version 2
Ernest Miller Hemingway was born in 1899 at Oak Park, a highly respectable suburb of Chicago, where his father, a keen sportsman, was a doctor. He was the second of six children. The family spent holidays in a lakeside hunting lodge in Michigan, near Indian settlements. Although energetic and successful in all school activities, Ernest twice ran away from home before joining the *Kansas City Star* as a cub reporter in 1917. Next year he volunteered as an ambulance driver on the Italian front and was badly wounded. Returning to America he began to write features for the *Toronto Star Weekly* in 1919 and was married in 1921. That year he came to Europe as a roving correspondent and covered several large conferences.

It should be apparent from the fact that we can tell these two texts apart—tell which one is discourse, and which a constructed text—that our choices among the options for arranging the information are neither arbitrary, nor just aesthetic devices to ensure variety, but have some communicative function, making discourse more readily comprehensible. (The first text is in fact comprehensible, but processing it is a much slower and more laborious affair.) Again, if we can understand the reasons for these choices, we may go some way towards explaining that strange feeling teachers have when reading a piece of written work in which every sentence is grammatically correct, and yet there is something not quite right. That *something* may well be to do with these choices.

As we do make important choices between alternative versions of sentences, even though each one is correct in itself, then in a succession of sentences, it is possible that the choice is being dictated by the sentence before, each one having a knock-on effect on the structure of the next. At first then, it would seem that this ordering of information is another instance of a formal connection between sentences in discourse. On closer inspection it turns out to be also contextual, dictated by what is going on in the mind of the sender and the assumptions he or she makes about what is going on in the mind of the receiver.

One way of understanding this is to view the discourse as proceeding by answering imagined and unspoken questions by the receiver. In this light, all discourse seems to proceed like a dialogue, even if the other voice is only present as a ghost.

Where and when was Ernest Hemingway born?
Ernest Hemingway was born in 1899 at Oak Park, a highly respectable
suburb of Chicago.
What did his father do?
(where) his father, a keen sportsman, was a doctor.
What was his position in the family?
He was the second of six children.
Where did the family spend their holidays?
The family spent holidays . . .

and so on. It should be clear, on reflection, that the order of information in
each answer is dictated by the question. In this sense we can say that the
structuring principle of all discourse is dialogue; but we will need to
examine the relationship between the word order and this dialogue more
thoroughly.

5.5 Information structure in discourse

There are in fact many interpretations and explanations of this strange
aspect of communication, just as there are many names given to the
phenomenon itself. Yet all interpretations, despite differences of terminology, agree that a prerequisite of the explanation is to divide each sentence
(or, more accurately, each clause) into two. There are various technical
terms for these two parts, and also differences of opinion as to where a
particular clause divides, but still, this much seems agreed: the clause has a
bi-partite structure, and the function of the choice as to what information
we put in which part is to enable us to bring different bits of information
into differing degrees of prominence.

One widely accepted explanation is that the ordering of information is
determined by the sender's hypotheses about what the receiver does and
does not know. With this interpretation we might divide information into
two types—that which the sender thinks the receiver already knows, and
that which the sender thinks the receiver does not already know—and label
these two types *given* information and *new* information respectively. Any
unit of information may of course change status as the discourse proceeds,
and what was new in one sentence becomes given in the next, precisely
because it has just been said. Indeed, communication might be defined as
the conversion of new information into given information, and a successful
communicator as a person who correctly assesses the state of knowledge of
his or her interlocutor. If we misjudge, and treat what is given as new, we
will be boring; in the reverse case when we assume the new to be given, we
will be incomprehensible.

A typical discourse, then, proceeds roughly as follows:

Given . . . New.   Given . . . New.   Given . . . New.

each given unit being already known by the receiver, or deriving from a preceding piece of new information. A boundary between the two types of information may well coincide with, or indeed define, the boundary of a language unit: a sentence, a clause, or a phrase. We can analyse our biographical sketch of Ernest Hemingway in this way, and explain why the second version 'felt right' and the first version 'felt wrong'. The first clause can be divided as follows:

Given	*New*
Ernest Miller Hemingway was born	in 1899 at Oak Park, a highly respectable suburb of Chicago.

The writer may well have assumed that most book buyers already know of the existence of a writer called Ernest Hemingway, and even if they did not before they picked up the book, they would already have seen his name on the cover before turning to read this biographical sketch inside. Even without previous knowledge or the sight of a cover or title, people often have to process new information at the very beginning of a discourse, though this is often mediated by a kind of meaningless dummy, like 'there was' in the given slot at the beginning:

Given	*New*
There was	a man called Ernest Hemingway.

The fact that Hemingway was born can be treated as part of the given information because all human beings are born (with disputable mythical exceptions). The next part, though, 'in 1899 at Oak Park' might reasonably be treated as new. Notice, before we leave this opening clause, how one piece of what is probably new information is slipped into the middle of the given information. It is unlikely that most readers already know Hemingway's middle name, but there it is, unobtrusively inserted. (This is a favourite technique of the advertiser and political propagandist.)

Next we have

Given	*New*
... where his father,	a keen sportsman, was a doctor.

we know he must have had a father, from our knowledge of the world, but we did not know what he was. (Notice how the stock opening 'X was born' excludes the main protagonist in this universal biographical event: the mother.)

Given	*New*
He was	the second of six children.

We already know Ernest existed, but not his position in the family.

Given	*New*
The family	spent holidays in a lakeside hunting lodge in Michigan, near Indian settlements.

We know he had a family—six of them have already been mentioned—but not whether they went on holiday nor where; although here we may make an important cultural assumption: if we assume it as a norm that families go on holiday, a fact of life as inevitable as having a father, we might divide it into

Given	*New*
The family spent holidays	in a lakeside hunting lodge in Michigan, near Indian settlements.

The ordering of given and new information is not always as straightforward as this, however. The very next sentence: 'Although energetic and successful in all school activities, Ernest twice ran away from home before joining the *Kansas City Star* as a cub reporter in 1917' departs from this pattern. New information is forced to the front as though it were given information, suggesting that a famous writer can always be assumed to be energetic and successful at school. (Alternatively we can read this as beginning with a clause in which the given is ellipted: 'although *he was* energetic and successful'.)

▶ TASK 33

Imagine a situation in which you have just marked 200 examination scripts. You might then be asked any of the following questions:

A What have you just done?
B How many examination scripts have you marked?
C Who marked these 200 examination scripts?
D What did you say you had marked?
E What have you done with these 200 examination scripts so far?
F When did you mark these examination scripts?

1 For each question give a short answer of between one and five words.

2 If your spoken answer to each question was the full 'I've just marked 200 examination scripts', which word or words would you stress in each case?

3 If you had written a full answer to each question, how could you have rearranged the word order to draw attention to the most important word or words?

These are not the only interpretations of the information structure of discourse. The two-part structure of each clause may reflect the way the sender has organized the information in her own mind, more than the way she guesses it is being received in another. Alternatively, the sender may wish to make certain parts of the message the *topic* of what she is saying—the focus of attention—and others simply *comments*. There may also be purely formal grammatical restrictions on what can go first. In fact, all these explanations may be true, and interact with each other to produce an incredibly complex, elusive, but very suggestive effect. So far, we have dealt with only the ordering of information in writing. In speech the situation is further complicated by the way stress and intonation can draw attention to any part of an utterance, and indeed this whole subject has traditionally been dealt with as an issue in the study of spoken language. No one fully understands the workings of these interlocking systems and we may forgive ourselves for having a sensation of something slipping through our fingers when we try to grasp them—but one thing is certain: the choices we make about the order of the information in discourse reveal our own assumptions about the world and about the people we are trying to communicate with. The truth of those assumptions gives unity to our discourse and success to our communication. Their falsehood puts it in danger of collapse.

▶ TASK 34

Account for each clause of the following newspaper report in terms of the writer's assumptions of what is given and new information for the reader. What problems do you encounter?

Yorkshire born climber Alan Hinks leaves for the Himalayas next week to take part in an historic assault on the Tibetan peak, Shishapangma. Alan, 33, will join renowned Polish mountaineer Jerry Kukuckza as he attempts to complete a remarkable sequence of conquests of the world's highest mountains. For the Polish climber, Shishapangma is the only mountain over 8,000 metres which he has yet to climb. There are fourteen in all. The only person to achieve the feat of all 14 8,000-metre peaks is the Austrian superman Reinhold Messner.
(*Yorkshire Evening Post*, 7 August 1987)

Show its structure as dialogue by inserting a 'ghost' question between each clause.

6 Knowledge in discourse

6.1 Introduction

We have frequently referred to the importance of world knowledge and social knowledge in the production and reception of discourse. Existing knowledge in the receiver of a message, and the correct assessment of the extent of that knowledge by the sender, are essential for successful communication. This is true of every approach considered so far.

Interpreting the cohesive devices described in 2, for example, depends upon the knowledge of the receiver, as in:

There was a pineapple on the table. I ate it.

where, to interpret the word *it*, we need to know that pineapples are edible and tables are not. Knowledge is also assumed in the functional views of language described in 3. When my neighbour said:

I'm sorry. I saw you were home. There's a cat stuck under the gate . . .

she assumed that I knew about the abilities and feelings of humans and cats, about houses, territory, and the socially stereotyped roles of women and men. Similarly, the sergeant, in issuing an order, could assume that Jones had knowledge of the authority of sergeants, the obligations of privates, the importance attached to polished boots on parade grounds, and so on. In 4 we saw how successful participation in discourses—whether in formal, institutionalized discourses like school lessons or informal discourses like conversations—depends upon pre-existent knowledge of how such events are likely to proceed and what sort of behaviour is appropriate at any point. Lastly, in 5, we have seen how the receiver's knowledge affects the ordering of information and thus the grammatical choices and word order of discourse too.

We need now to look more closely and more precisely at the role of knowledge, and how it interacts with language to create discourse.

6.2 Knowledge structures: schemata

In recent years the role of knowledge in discourse production and comprehension has been significantly stimulated by findings in the field of Artificial Intelligence, which, among other endeavours, attempts to program computers to produce and understand discourse. As we have seen, this involves far more than the language being used; it involves pre-existent knowledge of the world. Artificial Intelligence tries to understand how this knowledge and language interact, and to reproduce the process in computers.

For discourse analysis, the most important idea to come out of the field of Artificial Intelligence is that of knowledge *schemata*. These are mental representations of typical situations, and they are used in discourse processing to predict the contents of the particular situation which the discourse describes. The idea is that the mind, stimulated by key words or phrases in the text, or by the context, activates a knowledge schema, and uses it to make sense of the discourse. To program a computer to understand a discourse, Artificial Intelligence researchers need to repro-duce this process, and to give computers both the necessary language knowledge, and the necessary schemata. The suggestion is that computers can be programmed to process discourse in a similar way to human beings, though the complexity of human language competence and human knowledge are far greater than those of any existing computer.

How mental schemata operate in discourse production and comprehension is best illustrated by an example. Imagine a witness in a court case is asked to tell the court about her movements during the morning. She is asked to tell them everything: the whole truth. She begins as follows:

1 I woke up at seven forty. I made some toast and a cup of tea. I listened to the news. And I left for work at about 8.30.

Such a description might well be enough to satisfy the court. But suppose the witness had said:

2 I woke up at seven forty. I was in bed. I was wearing pyjamas. After lying still for a few minutes, I threw back the duvet, got out of bed, walked to the door of the bedroom, opened the door, switched on the landing light, walked across the landing, opened the bathroom door, went into the bathroom, put the basin plug into the plughole, turned on the hot tap, ran some hot water into the wash basin, looked in the mirror . . .

Although this is also true, we might not be surprised if the judge interrupted this witness and accused her of being facetious, or told her not to waste time. Why? How does the witness assess the amount of detail required? And if the court wants to know 'the whole truth', why do they want any details omitted? There is in fact an infinity of extra detail that could be added, even to the second version. (The witness did not mention every time she blinked, for example, or the fact that she was breathing.)

The point is that the second version contains superfluous and irrelevant information, though this would not necessarily be the case if we were explaining what we do in the morning to an (English-speaking!) Martian. It is not that the information in the second version is not true, but rather that it is assumed—and that the witness can assume it is assumed. Once she tells

us that she woke up and then that she prepared breakfast, we assume
certain facts: that she got out of bed, for example. When she tells us that she
left for work, we assume that she has dressed for the outside world. We
have knowledge of a typical 'getting-up in the morning', and we use it to fill
in missing details. This pre-existent knowledge could be called a 'getting-up
schema'. When a sender judges her receiver's schema to correspond to a
significant degree with her own, she need only mention features which are
not contained in it (the time of getting up and what she had for breakfast,
for example); other features (like getting out of bed and getting dressed)
will be assumed to be present *by default*, unless we are told otherwise.
(That is why it seems more reasonable to say 'I went to work in my pyjamas'
than 'I went to work in my clothes'.)

▶ ## TASK 35

Look again at the first version of the witness' testimony and answer
the question: What did she eat for breakfast? (This may seem
silly!—but read on.)

6.3 Evidence for schemata

There are a number of pieces of evidence that the mind does in fact employ
knowledge schemata in the interpretation of discourse.

One piece of evidence is the fact that people questioned about a text or
asked to recall it, frequently fill in details which they were not actually
given, but which a schema has provided for them. What did the witness eat?
The answer is that she did not tell us. She told us that she *made* some toast,
but not that she *ate* it. In reading this short passage we are likely to make an
assumption: that when someone makes breakfast, it is eaten. As nobody
else is mentioned we assume that the speaker ate the breakfast herself. But it
does not say this.

A second piece of evidence is provided by certain uses of the definite article.
Traditional grammars give two main explanations of the use of the definite
article (*the*) rather than the indefinite article (*a, an*): the former is used
before nouns referring to something unique, or before a noun which has
become definite as a result of being mentioned a second time. A typical
instance of the second of these rules is:

'One afternoon a big wolf waited in a dark forest for a little girl to come
along carrying a basket of food to her grandmother. (. . .) 'Are you carrying
that basket to your grandmother?' asked the wolf. The little girl said yes,
she was.'

But none of the rules given in traditional grammars can explain the use of
the definite article in an opening such as:

'I was late and we decided to call a taxi. Unfortunately, the driver spent a long time finding our house . . . '

Here the use of the definite article with 'driver' seems quite appropriate, even though he is mentioned for the first time. This is because our 'taxi schema' contains a 'taxi driver', and we assume that a taxi that arrives at our house has a driver. It is as though he has already been mentioned. We can test this by considering an alternative opening:

'I was late and we decided to call a taxi. Unfortunately, the retired admiral spent a long time finding our house . . . '

Now it might be the case that the taxi driver is a retired admiral; but we are unlikely to assume, without evidence, that our receiver already knows this. We would need to say so.

'I was late and we decided to call a taxi. The driver, as it turned out, was a retired admiral, and unfortunately he spent a long time finding our house . . . '

Further evidence for schemata is provided by the next task.

▶   TASK 36

Suggest a continuation for each of the following:

1 She's one of those dumb, pretty Marilyn Monroe type blondes. She spends hours looking after her nails. She polishes them every day and keeps them . . .
2 The king put his seal on the letter. It . . .

Now look at these continuations:

1 . . . all neatly arranged in little jam jars in the cellar, graded according to length, on the shelf above the hammers and the electric drills.
2 . . . waggled its flippers, and caught a fish in its mouth.

Interpretation of words with more than one meaning (like *nails* or *seal*) is determined by the schema activated to make sense of the discourse (Lehnert 1979:80). Our 'Marilyn Monroe' schema is more likely to include fingernails than the kind you knock into walls, and our 'king schema' will contain seals for stamping wax rather than the kind that eat fish. The schema activated by the opening leads to one interpretation of 'nails' and 'seal'—a phenomenon referred to in Artificial Intelligence as *expectation driven understanding*—and the schema is upset by an unexpected continuation, probably making you reread. There is a conflict here between ease of processing and interest. Surprises are harder to process but more interesting. That is why activating and then overturning schemata is a device often used in jokes, puzzles, and literature.

▶ TASK 37

An old man took his grandson out for a walk one day. While they were out walking the boy was hit by a car. An ambulance was called and the boy was rushed to hospital. At the hospital, a surgeon was called and the boy was taken immediately into the operating theatre. On seeing the boy, the surgeon immediately exclaimed, 'Oh my God! That's my son!'

1 What was the relationship between the surgeon and the boy?

2 If you do not have the same answer as the one at the end of **6**, what does this reveal about the schema you employed to interpret this discourse?

6.4 Complex schemata

Not surprisingly, considering the complexity of the interaction of minds, language, and the world, the description we have given so far is highly simplified. Actual discourse is unlikely to be interpretable with reference to a single schema. In reality the mind must activate many schemata at once, each interacting with the other. It must be capable of moving rapidly from one to another, of using more than one simultaneously, of focusing on a sub-schema (say a 'menu schema' within a 'restaurant schema'). It must be capable of building new schemata, and of ditching old ones.

What is more, schemata need not be limited to unordered catalogues of people and things within a stereotyped situation, or stereotyped sequences of events telling us what is likely to happen next. They may also predict stereotypical roles and relationships of participants, or they can be stereotypical text types, predicting plot structure or conversational development. Looking back at **4**, we might surmise that teachers and pupils have a shared schema for the progress and structure of a school lesson and their roles and responses to possible events. Similarly, participants in conversation have certain—no doubt highly culture-bound—assumptions about possible courses for a conversation, length and type of turn, total duration, and so on. Less reciprocal discourse will also activate schemata. When we watch a TV police thriller, we match it against a schema which contains certain characters, playing particular roles in certain sequences of events, in a plot with certain episodes and a particular outcome. Our pleasure (or displeasure depending on our taste, or mood) will derive either from the high degree of conformity of the individual example to the schema, or from its divergence.

▶ TASK 38

Describe the flat or house in which you live.

1 Can you identify features which you have assumed a receiver of your description will assume to be present by default (i.e. features

of the building which do not diverge from what you presume to be shared between your 'building schema' and a potential receiver's)?

2 In a series of experiments in which people were asked to describe their flats, Linde and Labov (1975) found that almost all subjects followed the order of describing the entrance, and then rooms branching off the entrance, returning to the hallway when they came to a dead end. Only after describing all rooms would they then proceed to detail their contents. Their descriptions, in other words, seemed to follow a set pattern, which we would describe as a 'schema for describing one's home'. Did your description follow this pattern?

3 Even in quite simple description we may adopt certain narrative patterns. Van Dijk (1977:80) suggests that we tend, for example, to move from the general to the particular; the whole to the part; the including to the included; the large to the small; the outside to the inside. Did your description conform to this prediction?

6.5 Relevance

Schemata, then, are data structures, representing stereotypical patterns, which we retrieve from memory and employ in our understanding of discourse. The successful communicator selects just those features which differ from this schema, enabling the receiver to adjust it and to bring it closer to the individual instance which is being described.

Schema theory can go a long way towards explaining the sender's choice and arrangement of information in communication. It can also elucidate some of the vaguer notions of pragmatic theory. One of Grice's maxims tells us to 'be relevant'—but it does not attempt to explain the notion of relevance. Speech act theory, by attempting to single out the pieces of shared knowledge which enable us to interpret the function of what is said, also assumes that we can distinguish which factors in the situation are relevant, but again it does nothing to explain how we distinguish the relevant from the irrelevant. Sperber and Wilson (1986) have used a model of communication which is very closely related to schema theory to explain the concept of relevance. Human minds, they say, have a long-term aim: to increase their knowledge of the world. In each encounter with discourse, we start with a set of assumptions, whose accuracy we seek to improve. Information is relevant when it has a significant effect on our assumptions: in other words, when it will allow us to alter our knowledge structures to give us a more accurate representation of the world. On the other hand, successful communication must work within the framework of the receiver's existing knowledge; it must not make too many demands. So relevant information adjusts our picture of the world very subtly. It is, say Sperber and Wilson, information which yields the greatest change in our knowledge for the least processing effort. Successful communication gives us new information, but works within the framework of the receiver's assumptions.

Schemata allow human communication to be economical. It would be hard to see how communication could take place if we could not take some sort of mutually shared knowledge for granted, if every discourse had to begin from scratch. The idea of pre-existing schemata will thus explain Grice's other maxims too. If we provide information which is already known to the receiver, then we are too long-winded; if we take knowledge for granted, we are too brief. In either case we violate the maxim of brevity. Communication also suffers when people make false assumptions about shared schemata, and it is then that they cease to 'be clear'. Lastly, our perception of the truth of discourse is also a comparison of the schemata it evokes—its assumptions—and our own.

Misjudgements and mismatches of schemata are particularly likely when people try to communicate across cultures and across languages. The resulting misunderstandings are endemic in the foreign language class-room. For this reason schema theory is of as great importance in language teaching as it is in discourse analysis.

6.6 Discourse deviation

Trying to understand the process by which two or more people come together through text to create discourse and thus communicate can be a very stimulating and exciting investigation. But there are also times when it can seem depressing. Increasingly, we seem to be talking about the unity and meaningfulness of discourse in terms of conformity: to another person's view of the world, to shared stereotypes. If communication is characterized as a successful attempt to alter the mental state of another human being, it seems that the most successful communication will take place where there is already a considerable coincidence between mental states, and the alteration achieved is only minimal. People who see the world differently, and therefore need to communicate, both for mutual education and to avoid conflict, may seem the least likely to be able to do so.

What happens to those who step outside the predictable patterns and regularities? Strangely, some are vilified and some are glorified. Some are called mad, disturbed, maladjusted, rebellious, even criminal; others are called individualists, poets, comedians, philosophers. It is easy to escape this issue by saying that the discourses of the two groups have little in common; but discourse analysis should teach us that it is as likely to be our attitude to what they say that categorizes them. Yet however we may judge deviation, whether negatively or positively, being a social outsider is very much a case of non-conformity to the norms and regularities of discourse structure.

Language learners are social outsiders of a different kind, standing outside one community by virtue of belonging to another. They may fail to understand or to make themselves understood because they lack the social knowledge which enables them to make text into discourse in the language they are learning. They may come out with oddities, and again we may judge this negatively or positively. The discourse strategies of a foreign speaker may seem refreshing exactly because they do not conform to conventions of the culture whose language they are learning; on the other hand they may cause serious misunderstanding and breakdown of communication. The task of the language teacher is a difficult one: to facilitate a degree of socialization which will enable learners to send and receive text as discourse, while also guarding their right to be different and to enrich others through that difference, bringing to the language they are learning the wealth of their own individuality and culture. As in the case of deviation within the social group: we do not have to judge difference negatively.

Success in communication depends as much upon the receiver as on the sender. Between speakers of different languages it depends as much upon the native speaker as on the foreign learner.

6.7 Conclusion

We started this book with a quest. We set ourselves the task of uncovering the principles behind our feeling that certain stretches of language are meaningful and unified: that they have the quality of coherence. We have explored a number of approaches which each give a partial answer to that question. In the course of this exploration, we have seen how much more is needed in the creation and understanding of coherent discourse than knowledge of the language system alone: its sounds and letters, its words and its sentence grammar. We have seen how coherence is created by our interaction with the text and is jointly created by both sender and receiver. But the various approaches are so far rather fragmentary. We have yet to integrate them one with another, and we have yet to relate them to the practical demands of learning and teaching foreign languages. These will be our aims in the next two sections.

Answer to Task 37: mother

Demonstration
Discourse in language learning and teaching

7   Two approaches to developing discourse skills

7.1 Introduction

In Section One we surveyed the major approaches to discourse analysis. We need now to turn our attention to existing exercises and activities for the language learner, and to assess the degree to which, by taking discoursal factors into account, they can help to develop effective communication. Attention to discourse does not necessarily entail sacrificing the traditional emphasis on pronunciation and writing, grammar and vocabulary. These are essential elements in communication, and discourse is realized through them. It is not even a question of reducing the time spent on formal aspects of the language system and squeezing them up to make room for a newcomer. Discourse and formal skills are interdependent and must be developed together.

7.2 A top-down approach to discourse processing

In Section One we took a bottom-up approach to discourse, and indeed to language as a whole (see Figure 8). Taking the so-called lower levels of language to some extent for granted, we proceeded from the most detailed features of discourse towards the most general. We looked first of all at the relationship of grammar to discourse and the extent to which formal cohesive ties operate across sentence boundaries. With that behind us we moved on to the interaction of language and context which defines language function; to the possibility of establishing overall structures of discourse related to particular discourse types; and to conversational mechanisms (although they might also be regarded, like cohesion, as formal devices linking smaller units). Lastly we looked at the way in which the form of words is affected by the sender's knowledge and idea of the receiver's knowledge. All these levels may be seen as controlled by the relationship of the people involved in the discourse, which we may regard as the highest level. This bottom-up approach may well be a very fruitful way of trying to understand what language is and how it works, but that does not mean that it is the best way to teach a language, or that it is the way we use a language when we do know it.

Figure 8

▶ TASK 39

The following are a list of possible activities to aid students in discourse comprehension. Arrange them in a top-down sequence.

- identifying the meaning of pronouns
- predicting the contents
- answering factual questions
- practising grammatical structures
- identifying the sender and intended receiver
- scanning for information
- discussing issues raised
- defining words
- giving a title
- taking notes on a given topic

We can gain some insight into the relationship of these two approaches to discourse processing by considering how difficult English discourse appears to students. As competent users of English, it is not easy for us, when looking at a piece of discourse which we understand, to imagine how it appears to the language learner. Teachers who have themselves learnt English as a foreign language may cast their minds back to an earlier stage in their own development; experience of learning other languages may also provide some help. Another way of gaining insight into the students' predicament is to analyse how we ourselves (native and non-native speaker) set about tackling pieces of English discourse which pose comprehension problems for us.

▶ TASK 40

Read the following extract. How do you react to it? How do you think an advanced learner would react? Which of the questions below will reveal most about the reader's communicative competence?

Malone, the fourth quarterback to start a Steelers' opener in as many seasons, hooked up with Lipps for a 33 yard completion to the Colts' 18 yard line on the Steelers' third offensive play. Lipps then caught an 11 yard Malone pass before making a leaping seven yard touchdown catch over Colts' cornerback Preston Davis in the end zone. The Steelers made it 14–3 on Lipps' 11 yard scoring grab early in the second period. A bad snap on a Colts' punt attempt later gave Pittsburgh the ball on the Indianapolis 34 and Malone connected with Brenberg for the final Steelers' first half score with 1:03 remaining.

(*International Herald Tribune*, 9 September 1985)

1 Who (or what sort of person) is the sender of the message?
2 What sort of person is the sender addressing?
3 Where are the addresser and the addressee?
4 What is the purpose of the discourse?
5 Is this a complete discourse or an extract?
6 What type of discourse is this (e.g. letter, recipe, novel, report)?
7 What is the meaning of the following: *hook up*; *completion*; *touchdown catch*; *end zone*?
8 Which of the participants in the event was most successful?

Unless you happen to be a keen follower of American football, you are more likely to be able to answer the first six questions than the last two. You probably succeeded in realizing that this is an extract from a sports report designed to inform people familiar with the sport about the progress of a match, and that the whereabouts of sender and receiver are not of particular importance. When we set about trying to understand difficult discourse we often start with the kind of knowledge elicited by the first six questions. We know some general facts, and we can begin to fill in the gaps in our understanding. A student, faced with discourse slightly beyond his or her current knowledge, is in the same position relative to that discourse as we are to the above. We should expect a student to tackle a problematic discourse in the same way as we would ourselves: that is to say top-down, starting with general ideas of the discourse and filling in details—like difficult word meaning—later. To ask about details before establishing the general context is to approach from the wrong direction. It can also cause panic and despair.

Task 40 demonstrates that we do not approach difficult discourse in our own language by starting at the bottom levels and then patiently working our way towards the top and a general understanding of what is being said. Rather, we take some linguistic and situational detail as a cue, form a general hypothesis and then try to build into that scaffolding. Consider the predicament of native speakers watching a film with a bad soundtrack, or speaking to someone who talks indistinctly or in an unfamiliar dialect. They do not panic when they do not understand every word, and they certainly do not think there is a fault in their own language knowledge. They form a general idea and fill in the details.

It is the difference between drawing a picture of a wall brick by brick, as in
(A) in Figure 9, or filling in an outline, as in (B).

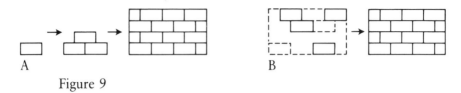

A   B

Figure 9

The second approach can be a very productive strategy in a foreign
language too. Human beings make general hypotheses about discourse, no
matter how little of the language they know. It is impossible, and it would
be foolish, to stop them doing so, for this is how competent language users
handle discourse. What we must help students to do is to formulate the
right hypotheses.

▶ TASK 41

In their book *Discourse in Action* in the series *Reading and Thinking
in English* Moore *et al.* (1980:x–xi) use the following sequence of
activities with reading comprehension:

– Prediction of contents based on the title, before reading the
   passage
– Extensive reading: skimming ('to identify important ideas');
   scanning ('to pick out points of detail')
– Intensive reading: questions helping students understand sections
   more closely
– Information retrieval: students are guided to use information for
   summaries, diagrams, and tables
– Evaluation: students express their opinions, compare the passage
   with others
– Follow-up: a challenging activity to make use of and extend the
   information.

To what extent does this sequence correspond to a native speaker's
processing of discourse? Is it a top-down or a bottom-up approach,
or a mixture?

7.3 Atomistic and holistic activities

A top-down approach to language regards all levels of language as a whole,
working together, while a bottom-up approach divides communication
into discrete levels, which can be dealt with separately. This separation of
levels may well have a role to play in the study and teaching of discourse,
and we shall need to think carefully about its role in language learning.

Communication is so complex an interaction of mind, language, and the physical world that it can be disconcerting to try to deal with it all at once. Yet we should not forget that communication does involve handling everything together, usually at high speed, and that this is what a successful language student must eventually be able to do. Splitting communication into levels may sometimes help, but those separate levels will always need to be reintegrated if communication is to take place. Sadly, this does not always happen.

A good deal of language teaching has followed a bottom-up approach, in that it has considered only the formal language system, often in isolated sentences, without demonstrating or developing the way that system operates in context. Even within the formal system, further divisions have been made, so that exercises, parts of lessons, and home assignments attempt to deal with pronunciation or vocabulary or grammar in isolation.

We can refer to this division of language into parts as an *atomistic* approach, and its opposite—an approach which involves all the parts working together—as *holistic*. There is a widespread assumption that atomistic activities should come first and holistic ones second. It appears in many guises, and persists even in the communicative approach, despite claims to put language skills in a subsidiary position to communicative skills. Rivers and Temperley (1978:4), for example, refer to two basic kinds of language learning activity: 'skill getting' and 'skill using'. Littlewood (1981:86) writes of 'pre-communicative' and 'communicative' activities.

▶ TASK 42

Consider the following sequence of activities around a reading passage in Roy Kingsbury's (1983) *Longman First Certificate Coursebook* Unit 21, entitled 'Daydreaming: This time tomorrow . . .'. Consider the extent to which the approach can be said to be atomistic or holistic, bottom-up or top-down.

– *Instruction:* students are told to read the passage, then do the exercises.
– *Reading passage:* a secretary's thoughts about her job (written in a 'thought bubble' beside a drawing of the secretary).
– *Exercises:* students decide if statements about the passage are true or false; in small groups, they list, discuss, and tell each other what the woman will be doing tomorrow, and what she will have done by 5.30; they then discuss the woman's feelings and decide what advice they would give her.
– *Grammar exercises* (each preceded by examples and statement of rule) on various verb forms occurring in the passage.

▶   TASK 43

Here is a sequence of activities around a reading passage from Simon Greenall's and Michael Swan's (1986) *Effective Reading* Unit 20, entitled 'Save the jungle—save the world'. Activities are grouped under a number of headings.

- *Predicting:* students look at the title of the passage and discuss their expectations in pairs; they then write down ten words they expect to find; they then read the passage and see if their words appear.

- *Extracting main ideas:* students choose one of six statements which gives 'the most accurate summary of the passage as a whole'; they decide who is responsible for the destruction of the jungle from four alternatives; they then read the passage again and make notes on how to save the jungle.

- *Dealing with unfamiliar words:* students look for words and phrases which are defined in the passage; find typographical indicators of explanation; indicate whether listed words from the passage have a positive or negative connotation.

- *Linking ideas:* students identify the meaning of selected cohesive devices in the passage; they then answer factual questions about the passage.

- *Understanding writer's style:* students discuss the meaning and the reasons for given stylistic choices.

- *Further work:* students prepare 'a similar document' on related issues.

Again, consider the extent to which the approach is atomistic or holistic, bottom-up or top-down. Compare this with the approach in Task 42. Decide which you think is most effective.

7.4 Arguments for and against an atomistic approach

Many students, teachers, educationalists, and examiners like to deal with things which can be classified as clearly right or wrong, and perhaps this is one reason why they have favoured an atomistic approach to foreign language learning, for communication is hard to assess, whereas isolated levels like grammar and vocabulary are much easier. Another reason is perhaps sheer incredulity that anyone can gain control over the systems of language and communication operating as a whole. Only by reducing them to sharply defined and manageable areas, it is felt, can we ever begin to understand their systematic nature and operate their rules. Yet, amazingly, human beings do manage to do this. Infants developing competence in their first language, experience it as a working high-speed whole, yet acquire native speaker competence without any formal instruction, apparently without effort, without any conscious formulation of rules, and without any splitting down into manageable 'areas' (although the features of adult speech to children may provide some help). Foreign language students do not generally attain the same kind of competence as first language speakers, but they too manage to operate the systems of communication as a whole. They cannot have done this only by dividing the language into neat areas, for the areas interact in complex ways in which the whole is not equal to the sum of the parts.

Arguing from studies of first language development has serious limitations. There are important differences between native and foreign language acquisition and in the latter case there are valid arguments for a degree of atomism as an intermediate measure. Whatever disadvantage teenagers and adults may have with new languages, they have abilities which infants, for all their daunting ease of acquisition, lack. They can think *about* language, uncover its systematicity, think and talk metalinguistically. They can also gain control over their material through the productive learning strategy of dividing it into areas and then seeking to reintegrate them. Although some theorists, in their desire to reproduce the course of first language development, have scorned the relevance of these abilities to second language development, it seems foolish to take *no* account of them, especially as we cannot stop older students from seeking awareness of the rules governing the material they are trying to learn.

Many students, moreover, have their own ideas about how a language is best developed, and it may be counterproductive for a teacher to overrule them. They may feel discouraged at the magnitude of the task before them, and gain a sense of achievement and control by isolating parts and dealing with them thoroughly.

Another reason why language teaching has traditionally tended to be atomistic and bottom-up is that it has followed the historical development and procedures of linguistics. Some schools of linguistics have sought to understand language by isolating it from its context: something which is clearly impossible when we actually use language for communication. The aims and methods of linguistics are thus quite different from those of the language student, who needs to use the language, not to understand its internal workings. Atomizing language by approaching it bottom-up has yielded results for linguistics, but it does not necessarily follow that the same is true for all language students.

7.5 Conclusion

In Section One we were concerned with understanding the mechanisms of discourse for ourselves, and we approached the problem bottom-up. In this section, where we are concerned with the development of discourse skills in students and the degree to which existing materials help this development, we shall proceed in the opposite direction from that of Section One and move top-down through the levels of discourse described in Figure 8. We do this in the belief that this is how competent language users handle discourse and that this is the best way of approaching discourse at any level of language development. In 8 to 11 we shall deal with separate levels of student discourse processing and production. In 8 we shall discuss the social relationships and shared knowledge of senders and receivers; in 9 the role of discourse type, internal structure, and function; in 10 conversational management, and in 11 cohesion. Yet as each level involves all those beneath it, we must bear in mind, as we move down through them, that it is not possible to keep levels neatly separate. All levels relate to and interact with all others, and in 12, we shall consider activities which practise and develop this relationship.

8 Focusing on senders and receivers

8.1 Introduction

In language use (as opposed to the drills of formal language practice) we almost always have some sort of knowledge about the senders or receivers of the discourse. Sometimes, particularly in some types of written discourse, we have only a very general or limited knowledge. In the production or processing of discourse with a low degree of reciprocity (for example, a manual, a road sign, a circular letter) we can say very little about the individual identity of the person or persons in communication with us; their name, gender, age, personality, appearance, and so on. Nevertheless, we still make certain assumptions about them and about our relationship to them, otherwise we would simply not know how to orient ourselves towards the language, or what to say.

The implication of this for the language teacher is that it should always be ascertained that students know as much as necessary about the identity of the receiver or sender of discourse. Or, if they do not know enough, they should be encouraged to find out. The concentration of traditional language teaching upon literary texts and newspaper articles has perhaps lulled course designers, teachers, and students into a false sense of security. In such discourses, what can be specified about the sender is often justifiably taken for granted, because the student has experience of these discourse types in his or her own language: in the modern world we are unlikely to come across a student who does not have some idea of the nature of news or fiction, and the sort of relationship entered into with the senders. Yet there are many other kinds of discourse in which establishing the necessary detail about our interlocutor is more difficult. We have already seen in our analysis of speech acts (in 3) how the meaning of a simple piece of spoken discourse like *The window is open* can change fundamentally with the relationship of sender and receiver, and this feature of language is by no means peculiar to speech. Here we shall examine how we can help students ascertain that relationship and its effect on meaning.

► TASK 44

When asking students to produce discourse, do the materials you use take the effect of different receivers into account? Compare the attention paid to the supposed receiver in the following writing instructions from two textbooks:

Extract 1

> Below you can see a picture of a demonstration. Report this event, using the ideas beneath the picture to help you.
>
> The report should be in the past.

(Jolly 1984:84)

Extract 2

> IDEAS FOR LETTERS
> *Choose one of the following topics (. . .) and write a letter to a friend or close relative. Begin and end the letter in a way suitable to the person you are writing to.*
> a) An English friend wants to learn your language (or another foreign language). Write a letter detailing your experience in language learning, and explain what you think is the best way to go about it.
> b) A letter about an unusual party, visit or trip.
> c) A letter about a new job or a course of studies.
>   [Five more topics are given.]

(Coe, Rycroft, and Ernest 1983:15)

Writing or speaking tasks which do not clearly specify the receiver make even native-speaking students tongue-tied, and not surprisingly, for we simply do not talk or write into vacuums. Even on a crossed telephone line, listening at random to shortwave radio messages, or casting a note in a bottle on to the waves, humans always form some hypothesis about the sender or receiver. We need to know who discourse is for, often in detail. In Task 44 Extract 1, for example, we might need to know the political opinions, or temperament, or personal involvement of the person for whom we are writing a report of the demonstration; and in Extract 2, a friend with whom we correspond might be nine or ninety, someone we saw last week, or someone we have not seen for decades.

There is, it is true, growing acknowledgement of the need to specify senders and receivers for students. Here the influential Council of Europe publication *The Threshold Level in a European Unit/Credit System for Modern Language Learning by Adults* (van Ek 1975) set the tone for many subsequent language courses, specifying *social roles* and *psychological roles* as two of the main parameters with which students need to cope (the others are *settings, topics*, and *language functions*). Social roles are divided into two main categories:

– friend to friend
– stranger to stranger.

and other relationships are subsumed under the second of these categories, for example:

– private person/official
– patient/doctor, nurse, dentist.

Psychological roles are: *neutrality*, *equality*, *sympathy*, and *antipathy*.

8.2 Office, status, role, and identity

As we have already said, it is not always necessary to know very much about the individual identity of the sender or receiver, but only certain general facts about his or her social relation to us. Sociologists distinguish three factors in social relationship:

Office: a relatively permanent position within the social structure to which someone is appointed or qualified, for example, electrician, nurse, pilot

Status: a general term for social importance influenced by facts like age, wealth, education (and office), and varying relative to other individuals

Role: a temporary interactional stance, involving the performance of certain types of perlocutionary and illocutionary acts (see **3.14**) often dependent upon having a certain status and office.
(*Adapted from Gremmo, Holec, and Riley 1985:39*)

The three of course interact, and an example is the best way of elucidating the difference. Saying that someone is *a doctor* may refer to office, status, role, or all three together. Thus a person with medical qualifications has the office of doctor, wherever he or she is. In many societies this office confers status: though not necessarily (if the doctor is known to be guilty of malpractices, for example). Doctors do not always act out the role of doctor, which confers the right to open a consultation, to ask personal questions about health, to instruct us to do things, and to close the interaction fairly summarily. Office, status, and the possible roles they confer are highly culture variable and may need general discussion with students. Knowledge of these three parameters affects our interpretation of what is said, and should be clear to students. The meaning of 'Let me look into your eyes' is clearly affected by the office and role of the sender! (For a further discussion of role see Wright: *Roles of Teachers and Learners*, in this Scheme).

Knowledge of office, status, and role is sometimes all we need. When we write to a bank manager asking for an overdraft, we will probably take all three into account if we wish to succeed; but we do not need to know any other personal details. In a medical consultation, only the office and role of doctor need to be identified. In conversation with friends, however, we need knowledge of their individual lives as well as of their social identity. There is thus an interaction between the degree and the kind of information we need, and the discourse type and function.

▶   TASK 45

Using your own experience of job interviews, either as interviewer or interviewee, and before reading on, write down ways in which the status, role, and office of the participants affect the nature and development of the discourse. Then consider this invented dialogue from a language teaching textbook. Do you feel that it has successfully captured some of the effects of the social relationship?

MR RICHARDS: Good morning Mr Plant. Do sit down.
CHRISTOPHER: Thank you.
MR RICHARDS: First of all I'd like you to tell me a bit about what you've been doing.
CHRISTOPHER: Well, I left school after I'd done my A levels.
MR RICHARDS: What subjects did you take?
CHRISTOPHER: French, German and Art.
MR RICHARDS: Art?
CHRISTOPHER: Well, I really wanted to study art. But a friend of my father's offered me a job. He's an accountant in the City.
MR RICHARDS: I see. In your application, you say that you only spent nine months with this firm of accountants. Why was that?
CHRISTOPHER: Well to be quite honest, I didn't like it—so I got a place at the Art College.
MR RICHARDS: Did your father mind?
CHRISTOPHER: Well, he was quite disappointed at first. He's an accountant too, you see.
MR RICHARDS: Have you any brothers or sisters?

(Abbs, Cook, and Underwood 1979:49–50)

This dialogue, like others in the same book, is exploited in various ways. For example: students hear only half of the dialogue on tape and have to supply the missing lines; students take notes and then give an account of what happened; students act out what happened from memory; students answer questions about the dialogue. Do you think these activities will help students to develop an understanding of the effect of social relationships on discourse in English?

8.3 Shared knowledge

Apart from needing to know varying amounts about the office, status, role, and personal details of people we are communicating with, we also need to form hypotheses about the degree of knowledge we share with them and the degree to which the schemata they are operating correspond with our own. As we have seen in 5 and 6, this assessment affects every level of discourse, from the quantity and ordering of information, to cohesion, the use of the article, and grammatical structure. Discourse which underestimates the degree of existing knowledge becomes boring; discourse which overestimates it becomes incomprehensible.

▶ TASK 46

The following extract from a language teaching textbook is supposed to be a conversation between two British children. Delete any information which you think the two children would have in common. Is this passage interesting? What pedagogic function does it have?

Pete: Do you like autumn Bob?
Bob: No I don't. It's a dull season. The grass is yellow. The leaves fall from the trees. If often rains. It's often cold. I like winter and summer. In summer the days are longer and warmer and the nights are shorter than in autumn.
Pete: But I like autumn. I think it's a beautiful season. I like to go to the forest in autumn. It's so beautiful! You can see all colours in the forest in autumn—the leaves are green, yellow, red and brown. There are lots of fruit and vegetables in autumn: apples and pears, plums and grapes, carrots and cabbages, cucumbers and tomatoes. I think it's a very tasty season!
Bob: And what about spring? Do you like it?
Pete: Oh yes, I like it very much, too. The leaves of the trees are small and green. The grass is green, too. It's warm in spring. I think that all seasons are wonderful.

(*Vereshchagina and Pritykina 1984:38–9*)

How could such a passage be used to develop discourse skills in the classroom?

8.4 Information quantity and ordering

We need then to consider activities which can develop student sensitivity to the quantity and ordering of information for a particular receiver.

Not surprisingly, as successful communication involves the transfer of information, and that transfer presupposes a successful evaluation of what is known and not known at the outset, a number of general suggestions have been made by theorists and methodologists advocating a communicative approach. Littlewood (1981) suggests a number of 'information gap' activities, where one student has information which others do not. Picture dictation and giving routes from maps are well-known examples of such activities. Long and Porter (1985) suggest an important division of such activities into 'one-way' communication tasks in which one student has exclusive knowledge of the information, and 'two-way' activities in which there is an exchange. Anderson (1985) suggests that when one student has information to impart, some of that information should be distributed among the other students so that a certain amount of negotiation can take place as to what needs communicating and what does not (see also Anderson and Lynch: *Listening*, in this Scheme).

All these activities will develop both processing and production of discourse by orientating students towards the knowledge of their interlocutor, and they are well documented in the literature of the communicative approach. But an information gap is not necessarily the same as the operation of different schemata, which may be working at a deeper and less accessible level. Moreover, these activities are interactions between students, and as such may fail to alert them to the choice and ordering of information produced by native speakers. In addition to general inter-student activity to promote communication, we need activities which will sensitize students to the way information is handled in discourse outside the classroom, but without using the kind of technical language we used in our theoretical approach in Section One. As there are at present few materials focusing on this aspect of discourse, the remainder of 8 suggests what such relevant activities might be.

8.5 Adding and removing information

We may take a piece of existing discourse, and add more information into it; then instruct students to remove surplus information in order to pitch the discourse for a specified receiver. Taking, for example, the biographical sketch of Ernest Hemingway which we analysed in **5.4**, we might expand it as follows:

'Ernest Miller Hemingway was born indoors in 1899 at Oak Park, a highly respectable suburb of Chicago, a large city in the USA, where his father, a keen sportsman, was a doctor. He was the second of six children. For short periods each year, the family spent holidays in a lakeside hunting lodge in Michigan, near Indian settlements. They spent the time there swimming and walking, and when the holidays were over they used to return home. The young Ernest, who grew older as the years passed by, attended a local school, and although energetic and successful in all school activities, he twice ran away from home, though he returned on both occasions. When he left school, he joined the *Kansas City Star* as a cub reporter in 1917. At that time there was a war raging in Europe, and the next year he volunteered as an ambulance driver on the Italian front and was badly wounded during an attack by the enemy army. This prevented him from continuing his work. Returning to America he began to write features for a newspaper called the *Toronto Star Weekly* in 1919, and in 1921 was married of his own free will to a woman he had met and fallen in love with earlier. That year he came to Europe by boat as a roving correspondent and covered several large conferences. He ate food every day and slept at night.'

We might then ask students to rewrite the passage, removing superfluous information. (This is also a constructive way to use the dull dialogue in Task 46.) There are several points to be noted about this exercise, however. First of all, it is of course essential to give the students specific information about the receiver(s), and indeed we can specify different receivers for different students. Secondly, we should note that the adding of information is not the same here as expanding units omitted through ellipsis (see **2.7**); nor is it the same as tautologically duplicating elements included in the meaning of words and saying, for example:

His mother was a woman.

Lastly, we might note the apparent similarity of this exercise to the traditional exercise of *précis*, the shortening of texts. Précis, however, does not specify particular receivers or adjust the information content to them. It is the shortening of a passage for general consumption, and aims to maintain the same information content, but to express it more economically.

▶ TASK 47

    1 How might the information in the Hemingway biography vary if addressed to: a child; the mayor of Oak Park; Hemingway's mother; an inhabitant of the 'Indian settlements' in Michigan; a Martian anthropologist?

    2 How could these changes be incorporated into an exercise for students?

8.6 Developing article choice in discourse

A second aspect of discourse which is partially conditioned by the degree of mutual knowledge and shared schemata is the use of the definite or indefinite article. Here again there can be no absolute criterion for choice if the discourse is divorced from its receiver. It is the attempt to deal with the choice as a formal rather than contextual issue which has led pedagogic grammarians into such easily flawed formulations of rules. As an exercise for students we can alter all or some instances of the article and then ask them to rewrite the discourse: again—as always—for a specified receiver. We should take care to distinguish between instances of the definite article which are textually determined by a previous mention and those which are determined by assumptions about the schemata of the receiver. Interestingly, in our Hemingway passage, there are no definite articles conditioned by previous mention—although the mention of a father and six children might justify the use of *the family*. The newspaper names have a definite article because there is only one.

▶ TASK 48

Compare the following version with the original in **5.4**.

Ernest Miller Hemingway was born in 1899 at Oak Park, the highly respectable suburb of Chicago, where his father, the keen sportsman, was the doctor. He was a second of the six children. The family spent holidays in the lakeside hunting lodge in Michigan, near the

Indian settlements. Although energetic and successful in all the school activities, Ernest twice ran away from a home before joining a *Kansas City Star* as the cub reporter in 1917. Next year he volunteered as the ambulance driver on an Italian front and was badly wounded. Returning to America he began to write the features for a *Toronto Star Weekly* in 1919 and was married in 1921. That year he came to Europe as the roving correspondent and covered the several large conferences.

1 For each change, can you specify receivers with particular knowledge or lack of it for whom the new use would be correct?
2 Which words or phrases here have changed meaning as a result of the article change?
3 How could these changes be incorporated into an exercise for students?

8.7 Adjusting information structure

The third aspect of discourse which is affected by the sender's assessment of the receiver's schematic knowledge is information structure (see **5.5**). It is possible to destroy the coherence of a discourse by altering its information structure (as we did in Task 32), and then ask students to restore its coherence for a specified receiver, but this may cause problems. Firstly, it is hard to explain what is required, and secondly jumbling sentence perspectives is also likely to involve the complex forms of the English clause. The explicit theoretical approach which we adopted in **5** should certainly not be necessary (unless our students are students of linguistics!), but we will need to give examples of alternative ways of ordering information in an English clause (as we did with the *John ate fish and chips* sentence in **5.4**) and then rely on the students' ability to acquire a sense of which is contextually most suitable. Bearing in mind these limitations, however, the activity has potential for improving the coherence of student discourse.

8.8 Changing between dialogue and monologue

Another way in which we sought to understand the nature of information structure in **5** was by saying that written discourse with a low degree of reciprocity proceeds as though answering a series of 'ghost' questions. It is like a dialogue with one half omitted. This fact has the potential to generate two further kinds of exercise which will develop this aspect of coherence: the conversion of

1 *dialogue→* into *→monologue*
2 *monologue→* into *→dialogue*

We shall return to these classroom activities involving the adjustment of information structure and the conversion of dialogue and monologue in **13**.

9   Discourse type and discourse part

9.1 Introduction

Continuing our top-down approach, we shall consider here the next three levels in Figure 8: discourse type and the closely related levels of discourse structure and function.

Far from being an academic abstraction, the notion of discourse type is something we all use every day in order to orient ourselves towards the communication in which we are involved. Languages abound with names for discourse types, and in English there are a good number of quite ordinary words, for example:

recipe	*joke*	*anecdote*	*label*	*poem*
letter	*advertisement*	*report*	*message*	*note*
chat	*seminar*	*manifesto*	*toast*	*argument*
song	*novel*	*notice*	*biography*	*sermon*
squabble	*consultation*	*sign*	*essay*	*jingle*
speech	*story*	*article*	*warrant*	*ticket*
lecture	*manual*	*cheque*	*will*	*conversation*
menu	*row*	*prescription*	*telegram*	*newspaper*

Such terms and their currency are another instance of the importance of top-down discourse processing. Tell somebody that 'It's just a joke', 'It's supposed to be a poem', 'No speeches please' or 'Let's have the meeting first and a chat later' and they will process or produce the discourse quite differently. There is no need to introduce any technical terms for discourse types, nor should we hesitate to name them to our students for fear of burdening them with jargon. They are a metalanguage, but one which exists in everyday language and is as useful for the foreign student as the native speaker.

► TASK 49

1 Group the above list of discourse types into categories in different ways. For example: *Chat* and *squabble* are both spoken and informal; *lecture* and *menu* both inform; *prescription* and *warrant* both depend on the sender's office.
2 Add more examples to your categories.
3 Pick out a few terms and decide how they are best defined.

4 Think of a group of foreign language students (either one you know or one defined by age, learning purpose, and situation) and decide which terms they will find most useful. In what order would you introduce them?

5 Do the materials you use differentiate in any way between discourse types?

Clearly, in some instances, there is a connection between discourse type and the office, status, or role of the sender and receiver (see **8.2**). Thus, although anyone can have a *conversation* or write a *poem*, it seems necessary to have a legal office of some kind to write a *warrant*. Similarly, one ought to have money to write a *cheque* or property to write a *will* (both features connected with social status). To make a *speech*, propose a *toast*, or write a *manifesto* is to take on a role and also to impose a role on the receivers. There is, however, no clear one-to-one relationship between discourse type and sender and receiver, and for many words denoting discourse type (*song*, for example, or *article*) we can make only the vaguest connections. There are, moreover, infelicitous instances of any discourse type. Quacks write *prescriptions* and bankrupts *cheques*. There are also complicating metaphorical uses of the terms too. Not all *lectures* are given by lecturers, or *sermons* by preachers.

Referring to instances of discourse types as *infelicitous* raises the issue of the relationship of these terms to speech acts and language functions (see **3.11**).

► TASK 50

Many textbooks, especially those published during the 1970s, divide material according to function. One such textbook has (among others) the following chapter headings:

– Talking about yourself (. . .)
– Asking for information (. . .)
– Getting people to do things: requesting (. . .) agreeing, refusing
– Talking about past events: remembering, describing experiences, speculating
– Offering, asking permission, giving reasons
– Giving opinions, agreeing, disagreeing
– Describing things, instructing people how to do things
– Making suggestions and giving advice, expressing enthusiasm, persuading
– Complaining (. . .), apologising
– Describing places and describing people
(*Jones 1977:v*)

1 What discourse types might realize these functions?
2 What is the nature of the relationship between function and discourse type?

With functions, as with senders and receivers, there is no simple one-to-one connection to discourse type. Though the function of a *menu* is usually to inform, it may also—left on a mantelpiece—serve to impress, to decorate, or to amuse. To say an *advertisement* has an advertising function begs many questions. Some advertisements may inform, others persuade, cajole, frighten, shock, worry, arouse. A *will* apparently has the function of bequeathing but it might also be intended to please or to repudiate—and to a historian, though that was not the intention, it may function as information. If even these apparently straightforward discourse types cannot be equated with single functions, what are we to say of *novels*, or *chats*, or *arguments*, or *jokes*? Function and discourse type, then, should not be confused. *To warn* is a function of language; but a warning may be realized in, for example:

– a letter ('I shall refer the matter to my solicitor.')
– a label ('Keep out of the reach of children.')
– a song ('You're gonna lose that girl.')

and so on. Functional courses which classify discourse by function alone often overlook this complex interaction.

▶ TASK 51

Many textbooks divide their material by discourse topic. The following are the chapter headings of one such book:

1 Teaching   6 Speech
2 Holidays   7 Jobs
3 The supernatural   8 Sports and games
4 Houses   9 Fashion and pop
5 Food   10 The arts
(Cook 1974)

1 What discourse types might be relevant to each of these headings?
2 What is the nature of the relationship between discourse topic and discourse type?

The point is that perception of discourse type is a factor in discourse processing and production which brings together our perception of sender/receiver, topic, function—and other factors besides. What is important from a pedagogic point of view is that we should, as early as possible, alert students to different discourse types, so that they may classify the interaction they are involved in, and make as productive a use of that classification as we do ourselves.

9.2 Culture specificity and discourse type

▶   TASK 52

Reading Resources (Forrester 1984) presents passages exemplifying the following discourse types: newspapers, fact sheets, details of consumer goods and services, advertisements, travel leaflets, dictionaries, and library catalogues.

Do you consider any of these to be culture specific: either because the genre does not exist in some cultures, or because it is substantially different?

Saying that we should teach terms for discourse types and encourage students to use them raises the issue of whether these types are specific to a particular culture. This is a difficult issue which entails the larger problem of the degree to which teaching a language is also teaching a culture. It is also one on which an enormous amount of research remains to be done. We might reasonably assume that some general categories are universal (*joke*, perhaps, and *song*), that others are shared between cultures which are close to each other in social history or organization (*bank statement, holy Koranic text, political street slogan, Christmas card*). From a pedagogic point of view, the possibility of culture specificity should alert us to the fact that when we teach terms referring to discourse type and use them in discourse processing and production, we should not take for granted that each term has an exact translation equivalent. Even in relatively close cultures, there may be important differences, perhaps the more dangerous for being slight. Among culturally heterogeneous students, or in classes where the teacher is from a different culture, there can be overt discussion of what students understand by different terms—of different styles and contents of jokes, for example, or the format of casual conversation. Many students enjoy such discussions and find them motivating. They are also culturally—as well as linguistically—educational, and if the much needed research into the cultural universality of discourse typology is to take place, the multicultural foreign language classroom provides excellent material. For the monocultural classroom, where students and teacher are from one culture, the situation is harder and must rely upon the teacher's understanding of the language and culture he or she is teaching.

9.3 Discourse type recognition

▶ TASK 53

In *Writing Tasks* Jolly (1984) has chapters headed *notes and memos*; *personal letters*; *telegrams, personal ads and instructions*; *descriptions*; *reporting experiences*; *writing to companies and officials*; *presenting facts and opinions*.

Which of these headings are in fact categories of discourse type? Does presenting them in this way, grouped in the separate chapters, aid discourse type identification?

Our recognition of discourse type employs every aspect of language and context. All or any of the following may be brought into consideration:

Feature	Example
1 sender/receiver	(technician, child, friend, employer, host)
2 function	(to obtain information; to attract attention)
3 situation	(at a party, on the factory floor, in a shop)
4 physical form	(folded piece of paper in envelope; large metal board)
5 title	(Air Ioniser Instructions)
6 overt introduction	(*Listen I want to tell you a joke; This is a story about*)
7 pre-sequence	(*Have you heard the one about; Once upon a time; Dear Kim*)
8 internal structure	(abstract + introduction + main text + book list + notes)
9 cohesion	(high frequency of logical conjunctions: *therefore, thus*)
10 grammar	(high frequency of subordinate clauses)
11 vocabulary	(archaisms, loan words)
12 pronunciation	(accent, volume)
13 graphology	(handwriting, print, type, dot-matrix letters)

Any of these may need to be present or indicated when students process discourse or are asked to produce it.

Many textbooks do show awareness of the need to deal with different discourse types, but few confront the issue of identification. To divide a book into chapters each dealing with a particular type is to sidestep the identification issue completely, yet it is still frequently done.

► TASK 54

One of the factors listed above as important in discourse type recognition is physical form. Consider the following examples from *Project English 2* by Tom Hutchinson and *Collins Cobuild English Course 1* by Jane and Dave Willis. How important do you consider the presentation of the original physical form? Is it important for discourse type recognition? Consider any other possible benefits. Are these discourse types culture specific?

Which video shall we get?

1 Imagine you have seen two of the videos. Write down the titles and when you saw them.

(*Hutchinson 1986:62*)

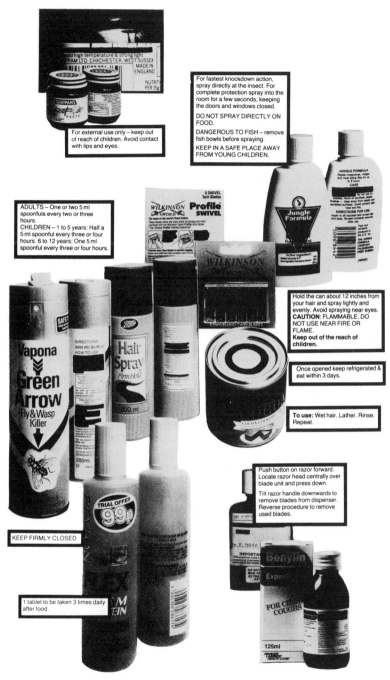

2 Parts of these labels are missing. Can you find a suitable label for
   each item?

(*Willis and Willis 1988:90*)

All instances of discourse have both a situation and a physical form, and this is often the main factor in our recognition of them. They do not suddenly appear out of nowhere or on the pages of a language textbook—which has much the same effect—but in varying sizes and on varying materials: out of ticket machines, on computer screens, under windscreen wipers, on hoardings. There are obvious problems for reproducing such features in the limited environment of the classroom, but wherever possible, perhaps, the physical form should be reproduced, or at least described. Many textbooks now do this with more than the usual letters, menus, maps, and newspaper cuttings (old favourites chosen as much for ease of reproduction as for their usefulness) and include pictures of cans and bottles and packets with legible labels, video covers, road signs, brochures, telex print-outs, and so on (as in Task 54). For example, *Reading Resources* (Forrester 1984) presents all the material (listed in Task 52) through photographs of the original physical form, as do other well-known compilations of authentic material like *Spectrum* (Swan 1978), *Kaleidoscope* (Swan 1979), *That's Life* (Duff 1979), and *Words!* (Maley and Duff 1976).

Such anthologies have great interest and value, not least because of their motivating appeal to students. Yet there may also be times when it is desirable to isolate the discourse from its physical realization and situation in order to concentrate upon other identifying features. Students may then be asked in what physical form and in what situation they would expect to find a given piece of discourse. Notice that it is possible to recognize and discuss the features of a discourse type without understanding it in detail—as is often the case, for native speakers, with legal documents.

▶ TASK 55

The book *English for Study Purposes* (Smith and Coffey 1982:35) gives the following instruction after a reading comprehension passage:

> Give a title to the passage. Choose the best alternative from the list below.
> A   Aerobic and Anaerobic Respiration
> B   Energy for Life through Respiration
> C   The Need for Oxygen
> D   Food as a Source of Energy

(Smith and Coffey 1982:35)

How useful do you consider this instruction? The choices here relate to discourse topic. Would it be possible to give choices of title which indicate discourse type as well?

As Task 55 suggests, another way in which discourse type can be recognized is by title. This may as easily refer to discourse type as to discourse topic (*Lecture notes on X*, for example, or *An article about Y*). Asking students to supply a title which refers to discourse type as well as topic, is a quick way of checking they have succeeded in orientating towards the discourse as a whole.

▶ ## TASK 56

In authentic discourse, titles sometimes serve to arouse interest by disguising rather than revealing either content or discourse type. The newspaper article in Task 34, for example, was entitled 'Double Top', in a punning reference to a score in the game of darts. Should students be discouraged from supplying such titles?

9.4 Orientation within a discourse type

Once students have identified the discourse type they are to process or produce, the next step is for them to 'find their way around' inside it. In **4.2** we discussed the way in which a hierarchical rank structure may be posited for various discourse types and considered as examples the internal structure of a series of books and a trial. Here again, there are many quite ordinary terms for the internal parts of discourse types.

▶ ## TASK 57

Consider the following extract which aims to help students find their way around the parts of a textbook. How effective do you consider this means of presentation and how widely could it be applied to other discourse types?

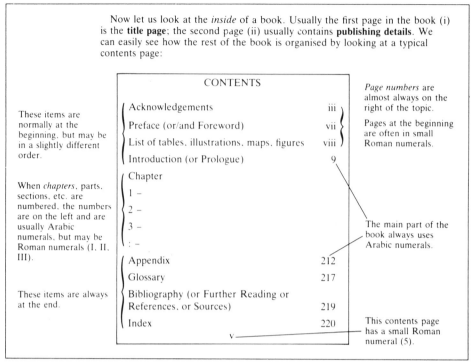

(*O'Brien and Jordan 1985:23*)

Now associate the following parts with particular discourse types, and consider how students could be helped to identify them and locate them:

headline	*introduction*	*list of ingredients*	*index*
chapter	*conclusion*	*summing up*	*notes*
lead story	*bibliography*	*editorial*	*title page*
vote	*salutation*	*instructions*	*date*
abstract	*address*	*glossary*	*proposal*

Do all discourse types have parts which are so easily named?

Where parts have names such as these, they should of course be used. Unfortunately not all discourse types, especially the less formal ones, have their own overt terminology, and we should avoid burdening students with the kind of specialized metalanguage employed in, for example, the analysis of a school lesson by Sinclair and Coulthard (1975) described in **4.3.** We should also be careful to distinguish between overt formal parts, which may well be labelled or explicitly stated in the original, and parts which discourse senders and receivers orientate to but do not label. A formal meeting may have stated stages, for example: *minutes of last meeting, proposal, seconding, amendment, debate, vote, reading of* *correspondence, any other business, closure*; but it is also possible to describe the parts as, for example: *routine business, heated debate, heckling*, and so on. Similarly, a novel may have labelled sections like *Foreword, Part I, Chapter 9*, and visible paragraphs; but it is also possible to recognize such parts as: *scene setting, character sketch, descriptive passage, dialogue, action, authorial comment*.

▶ **TASK 58**

As we have already seen, in Tasks 41 and 43, some books reverse the traditional order of text first then questions, to one of questions first then text. Books like *The Skill of Reading* series (eds. Ellis and Ellis 1982–4), *Looking for Information* (Jordan 1980), *Developing Reference Skills* (O'Brien and Jordan 1985), *Upgrade Your English* (Debska 1984), and many others all use prefaced questions like 'Look at these questions, *then* read through the passage quickly to try and find the answers' (*Skills for Reading* Morrow 1980:53).

How might such prediction interact with the identification of parts of a discourse? Do you think a successful prediction will entail knowing the parts of the discourse? How could this save a student time?

Parts within a discourse type, like the discourse type itself, may be recognized by a combination of the factors listed in **9.3**. The recognition and classification of parts is essential for effective comprehension. Native speakers do not read or pay equal attention to everything within a discourse. We gain little from minute attention to the manufacturers' congratulations for our choice of car, or from the swearing-in in court, and, on a first reading of a novel, it may be more important to follow those parts which forward the plot than those which set the scene.

For these reasons students must be able both to identify and find parts of the discourse and to avoid wasting time on minute and irrelevant detail. It is necessary both to predict what is likely to be found in a discourse before trying to process it, and to have a clear purpose in processing. In most encounters with discourse, especially written discourse, we are in some way prepared for what is coming, if only because we ourselves have sought it out with a clear purpose (Widdowson 1983).

In their introductions to the series *Reading and Thinking in English* (*Discovering Discourse* 1979:8; *Discourse in Action* 1980:3) Moore *et al.* argue for a preparation stage for all reading comprehension in which students should both predict what they expect to find in the discourse from

– the titles, subtitles, and their own knowledge of the topic
– the non-linguistic context: pictures, diagrams, etc.
– the linguistic context

and have a clear idea of the purpose of reading

– as part of their studies or occupation
– for a particular purpose in their daily activities
– for pleasure.

Their procedure with a text, then, would run as follows:

1 Contents	Individual	Students read silently. Teacher deals with problems.
2 Preparation and Abstract	Whole class	Teacher elicits information as a motivation to the unit topic or discourse type.
Expansion	Individual/ group/class or pair/class	Students work on activities on their own and compare conclusions in group discussion. The amount of time needed for discussion will depend on how open-ended the activity is.
3 Reading assignment		
Predicting the development		As expansion above.
Extensive reading	Individual/class	A quick check with the whole class should be sufficient.
Intensive reading	Individual	Deal only with recurring problems in class.
Information retrieval	Individual/class	Occasionally group discussion will be of value.
Evaluation	Individual/ group/class	Allow students to prepare the task individually.
Follow-up	Group	This may be followed by a brief class round-up.

(*Moore* et al. *1980:xvi*)

Within these general categories, precise predictions and purposes can be formulated and then checked or fulfilled, and exercises in skipping and scanning, finding facts or opinions, dividing and heading, paragraphing, and subtitling can all be entered into more purposefully.

▶ ## TASK 59

Do you consider the procedure from Moore *et al.* to be suitable for students of any age or level? If not, consider how it might be adjusted to different categories of student while preserving its efficacy as a means of encouraging orientation within a discourse.

Morrow (1980:Part 4) takes the subordination of text to purpose and prediction so far as to use the questions to construct the text (through a series of student activities like speed-reading of parts of the text, reordering, and blank-filling) while the text itself is hidden away at the back of the book for consumption afterwards. One of the techniques he uses here is to diagram the organization of the discourse in terms of topic and function, as shown in the extract below.

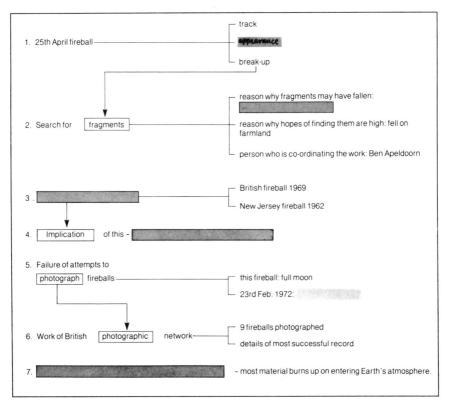

(Morrow 1980:92)

This use of diagrams enables students both to find their way around a text without losing themselves in the irrelevant detail of intensive reading, and also to identify parts without having to name them.

► TASK 60

Diagrams can be used in discourse production as well as in comprehension. Grewer, Moston, and Sexton (in Candlin 1981) give examples of discourse charts which can be used by learners to generate exchanges in particular contexts.

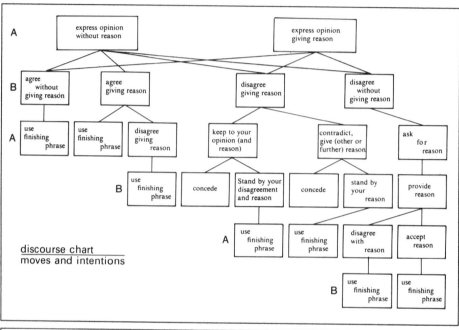

discourse chart
moves and intentions

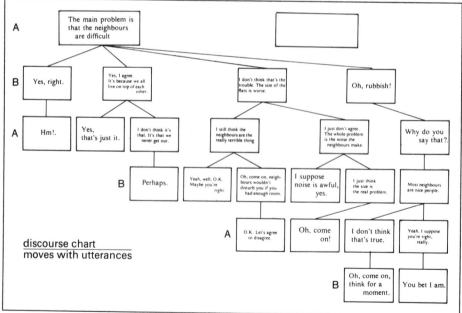

discourse chart
moves with utterances

(*Grewer, Moston, and Sexton, in Candlin 1981:154–5*)

Follow through the first of the above charts with a number of different contexts in mind and suggest alternative realizations like those in the second. What advantages or disadvantages are there in using this with students?

9.5 Orientation within a discourse part

Continuing our top-down approach to discourse, it is logical that having identified the sender and receiver, the discourse type and the parts within it, we should turn our attention to organization within parts of the discourse—however these may have been identified and defined. Here we begin to approach the level of cohesion (which we shall deal with in **11**), as well as the combination of clauses within sentences, and thus grammar, which is beyond the scope of this book.

Within the part, a functional analysis may take us further than at higher levels, for smaller units of discourse are more likely to be uni-functional, and transitions from one function to another may correspond to both overtly marked sections of the discourse like section, chapter, and paragraph, and also (indeed particularly) to sentences. Here again, a large amount of work has been done on the analysis of written discourse for students of ESP and EAP (see, for example, Selinker, Tarone, and Hanzeli 1981), but there is no reason why the same techniques cannot be applied more widely to the production and processing of writing of more general interest. (Spoken discourse, which happens in time only, poses different problems and is dealt with in **10**.)

The classification and relationship of functions within the discourse can again be represented diagrammatically, and students encouraged to think of discourse in spatial terms, as in the extract from Laird, where paragraph structure is analysed in functional boxes, each box corresponding to a grammatical unit or series of grammatical units.

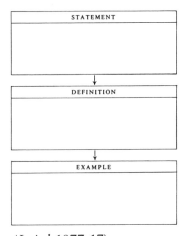

(*Laird 1977:17*)

Here again, as with discourse type and discourse parts, there are often quite everyday names for functions (as a glance at the contents page of any functional course will reveal), so there is no need to burden students with any metalanguage from the theory of discourse analysis.

9.6 Recombination, approximation, and transfer

Another activity which may draw students' attention to the organization within parts of a discourse is the well-known one of changing the order of sentences and asking students to put them back in their original order. This can alert students to paragraph structure and the position of topic sentences within it. It will also involve sensitivity to cohesion and the information structure of the clause. This exercise will be referred to as *recombination*.

We should note, however, that there is often more than one way of recombining sentences into coherent discourse and that the order is conditioned by the higher levels of discourse, such as the sender's perception of the reader's knowledge and interest, the function of the discourse, and its topic.

Two further activities which can focus students' attention upon the internal organization of discourse are *approximation* and *transfer*, proposed by Widdowson (1978:75–85), implemented in the *English in Focus* series (eds. Allen and Widdowson 1973–80), and adopted by many other writers since. Like the functional analysis of paragraph structure, these two activities develop awareness of both the higher levels of discourse organization and of lower levels like cohesion and clause combination.

Approximation involves the breaking down of a piece of discourse into a number of short isolated sentences, and then asking the student to combine them into a whole. Here, for example, is a short extract of scientific prose, which might well be relevant to a course in English for Academic Purposes (EAP).

'In contrast to the highly glandular skin of mammals, a bird's skin is nearly glandless. The only prominent external gland is located at the base of the tail and is called the *uropygial* gland. Its only secretion has been commonly regarded to be important in the care and waterproofing of the feathers. It is a fact that the gland is usually well developed in aquatic birds, where waterproofing is so essential, and that many birds appear to work the gland when preening their feathers.'

(Wesley Lanyon: *The Biology of Birds*)

We may break this down into a set of unconnected sentences containing the same information. One set of such sentences might be, for example:

1 Birds' skin contrasts with mammals' skin.
2 Mammals' skin is highly glandular.
3 Birds' skin is nearly glandless.
4 Birds have a gland at the base of the tail.
5 The gland is prominent.
6 The gland is external.
7 No other glands are prominent.
8 No other glands are external.
9 The gland is called the *uropygial* gland.
10 The uropygial gland has one secretion.
11 Scientists regard the secretion as important.
12 The secretion cares for the feathers.
13 The secretion waterproofs the feathers.
14 The uropygial gland is well developed in aquatic birds.
15 Waterproofing is essential for aquatic birds.
16 Many birds work the gland.
17 Many birds preen their feathers.
18 They perform the two actions at the same time.

▶   TASK 61

Consider the relationship between the sentences above and the original. Are there other possible sets of elementary sentences? Will a student be able to reproduce the original from them? Can other passages be created from them?

A number of points need to be considered. Firstly, there are different ways of breaking down the original discourse into what we shall refer to as *elementary sentences*. This is partly a question of how far we go in destroying the original unity. The most extreme breakdown would reduce the original to what philosophy and linguistics call *propositions*: representations of the most basic concepts of which the discourse is composed. Widdowson (1978:78) does use this term, but it is not necessary to go as far as this, or to know the linguistic and philosophical means of representing a proposition, and its nearest sentence equivalent. Teachers can reduce the discourse intuitively as far as they judge to be suitable for their own students. In fact, elementary sentences need not necessarily be derived from an existing piece of discourse at all. They may simply be invented, for although the act of invention may seem to depart from the current obsession with the use of authentic texts, we should remember that authenticity is a feature of how we use text, not of the text itself (Widdowson 1978:163–73). The process of combination with a specified receiver, discourse type, and communicative purpose approximates to authentic discourse production just as much as the use of sentences derived from an existing discourse.

Secondly, approximation involves not only orientation 'upward', towards the structure of the part and the discourse as a whole, but also 'downward', towards the choice of cohesive devices, the subordination and co-ordination of clauses, and the structure of information within the clause (see **5.4, 5.5, 8.7**). Approximation, in other words, is a further illustration of the impossibility of keeping an area of discourse separate from either other levels of language (grammar, vocabulary) or from other areas of discourse.

Thirdly, the exercise as proposed here—i.e. the combination of the elementary sentences into a piece of continuous discourse—is in fact extremely hard. Students may need guiding through stages of combination, perhaps with an indication of which elementary sentences are best combined into one, or with specific suggestions about cohesive and other combinatory devices. They move gradually towards a final version—hence the term 'approximation'.

▶ TASK 62

The *Focus* series contains a number of exercises asking students to study a diagram and then 'transfer' the information contained in the diagram into a continuous paragraph or vice versa.

1 Is there a connection between these exercises and those of approximation?

2 What relationship would a set of 'elementary sentences' have to the diagram and the piece of continuous prose?

We have seen how a set of elementary, single-clause sentences can be combined in many different ways according to context, receiver, and function, and how choice between cohesive devices varies with these parameters. The relationship of the discourse which is the final product of the exercise to this set of elementary sentences may be represented as in Figure 10.

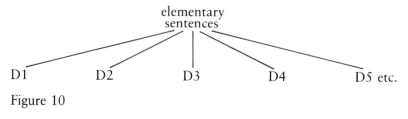

Figure 10

Here, discourses containing the same information are only related through the set of elementary sentences. It is equally possible, however, to move directly from one realization of the information to another without reference to any abstracted breakdown of content. We may now add connecting arrows (Figure 11):

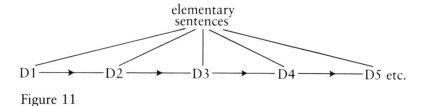

Figure 11

and dispense with the abstracted content, the elementary sentences, altogether. Any discourse type, moreover, may be transferred to any other (Figure 12):

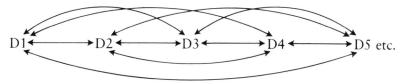

Figure 12

The transfer need not necessarily take place from one verbal realization of the information to another. In manuals, scientific texts, and many other cases, information is conveyed non-verbally, by means of charts, diagrams, and pictures. Students may be asked to convert verbal to non-verbal realizations of the same information and vice versa, a technique which is extensively used in the *English in Focus* series under the heading of 'Information transfer'.

► TASK 63

1 Are transfer exercises best suited to technical and scientific subjects which make extensive use of graphs, tables, and diagrams? Or are they applicable to any subject matter?

2 Are there any common and well-established language teaching exercises which are transfers of the same information from one discourse type to another, even if they are not usually called transfers? For example: *Towards the Creative Teaching of English* (Melville, Langenheim, Rinvolucri, and Spaventa 1980) asks students to convert mimes to stories; *Poem into Poem* (Maley and Moulding 1986) asks for poems to be converted to other discourse types. Are these transfer exercises? How do they differ from those described above?

In recombination, approximation, and transfer activities, we should note that there is no one correct way of combining information into a coherent discourse. Arrangement and choice between the various grammatical and cohesive options will be dictated by the way in which the discourse is intended to function and the context in which it is to be received. In this way the activities of recombination, approximation, and transfer form a link between the higher and the lower levels of discourse (Figure 13).

sender/receiver, type, purpose, structure
↑ ↑ ↑ ↑ ↑ ↑ ↑
recombination, approximation, transfer
↓ ↓ ↓ ↓ ↓ ↓ ↓
cohesion, grammatical and lexical choice

Figure 13

Any set of original or elementary sentences can be combined in different ways, according to whether the discourse is, for example, written or spoken, part of an academic article or a popular television show, whether the audience are adults or children, qualified biologists or beginners. No specialist discourse analysis terminology is needed. We can ask for the facts to be presented as
– a short talk for fellow students
– an explanation to a child
– part of an academic paper
and so on. The sentences function like a set of notes which may be realized in discourse in different ways. In this way students may acquire a range of *styles* determined by receiver, purpose, and discourse type.

The issue of stylistic variation during language development is undoubtedly a contentious one. Many approaches to language teaching implicitly take the view that it need concern advanced students only. What is needed to begin with, it is suggested, is a kind of bland neutral style with accurate grammar and vocabulary. Only when this has been achieved, should stylistic variation be considered: a kind of icing on the grammatical and lexical cake. A discoursal approach takes the opposite view: that there is no such thing as neutral style and therefore that stylistic choice and range need developing from the earliest stages. Stylistic choice is not an optional extra in communication, but one of its most important features. We have seen (**3.2**) how the social functions of language can outweigh its function in conveying information, and how (**5.4**), when the function *is* to convey information, an inappropriate style can impede it. When style is inappropriate, communication breaks down. Students need to communicate with different people in different situations and for different purposes. They need to make appropriate choices about the arrangement of information and devices for its combination, and to be sensitive to the implications of choices made by others.

10   Managing conversation

10.1 Introduction

A good deal of what we have said so far about the need for teachers and
students to pay attention to the higher levels of discourse can be applied to
both writing and speech. As we approach the 'bottom' levels, however, and
particularly as we begin to consider the internal structure of discourses and
their parts as we did in **9**, it becomes necessary to treat these different
discourses in different ways. Here we shall deal with the teaching of
conversational management, and also with the effect which cultural
differences may have on interaction, at both a local and a more general
level.

10.2 Spoken and written discourse

Spoken language, as has often been pointed out, happens in time, and must
therefore be produced and processed 'on line'. There is no going back and
changing or restructuring our words as there is in writing; there is often no
time to pause and think, and while we are talking or listening, we cannot
stand back and view the discourse in spatial or diagrammatic terms as we
did in **9.4**.

Nevertheless, despite these general observations about the difference
between spoken and written language, there are many types of speech
which *are* planned in advance or structured by custom and rule (like
meetings and *trials*). There are also many discourse types which are
intermediate cases between writing and speech: spoken language which is
read or learnt from a script (like *news bulletins* and *plays*) or based on
written notes (like *talks* and *lectures*). The range of possibilities can be
better represented by a cline than a sharp division. We should also
remember that the tape recorder and the video camera can to some extent
free the processing—if not the production—of speech from the domination
of time, and with their help it *is* now possible to go back over what was said,
and to pause and think about it too. And no longer can only
lightning-fingered stenographers transcribe it. (For a further discussion see
Bygate: *Speaking*, and Anderson and Lynch: *Listening*, in this Scheme.)

A further weakness in the traditional division of language into the two
major categories of speech and writing is that it disguises an even more
important division *within* the category of spoken language, between

'one-way' speech (for example, a *lecture*) and 'two-way' speech (for example, a *conversation*): a division, in other words, between speech with a high degree of reciprocity and speech with a low one (5.3). There are ways in which 'one-way' speech has more in common with writing than with 'two-way' speech.

So we can place instances of spoken discourse on one of the following clines:

      (1) planned ———— unplanned
    (2) socially structured ———— less socially structured
      (3) aided by writing ———— unaided by writing
 (4) less reciprocal (one-way) ———— more reciprocal (two-way)

Yet however we categorize spoken discourse, casual conversation as defined in **4.5** will be at one extreme. Conversation, being unplanned, relatively unpredictable, unaided by writing and involving frequent turn-taking, is different from other discourses, and needs a different treatment in the classroom.

▶ TASK 64

A teacher begins a class by saying: 'Today we are going to have a conversation about nuclear energy.'

1 List ways in which this opening deviates from the definition and description of conversation in **4.5**.
2 Would it make any difference if the teacher had called it a *discussion*, not a *conversation*?
3 What do you consider to be the differences between the discourse type *conversation* and the discourse type *discussion*?

10.3 'Teaching conversation'

Teaching conversation is notoriously difficult and can seem almost a contradiction in terms. The characteristic features of conversation include greater spontaneity and freedom, and a greater equality among participants than in other discourse types. All these features are at odds with the nature of the classroom, where language is directed towards a specific purpose, and where one person (the teacher) is traditionally in charge of the others (the students). The title of Penny Ur's (1981) book, *Discussions that Work*, reflects the widespread pessimism of teachers about talk in the language classroom. To write about discussions that work clearly implies that many do not. Yet if difficulty with 'conversation classes' is widespread, so too is the desire of students to converse successfully in the language they are learning. This is especially true in the contemporary world where chances of contact with native speakers are more likely.

▶ TASK 65

Teachers are usually the initiators of speech in the classroom. It has been said of grammar teaching that this teacher dominance results in students being able to use declaratives but not interrogatives, because they never ask questions.

What are the equivalent disadvantages of the teacher's role as instigator when students are developing their ability in conversation? How, for example, might the conversational behaviour of a student who needs or wishes to be assertive outside the classroom be adversely affected by being expected always to follow the teacher's lead inside it? Can you think of ways of overcoming this problem?

Conversation, as we have seen in **4**, involves far more than knowledge of the language system and the factors creating coherence in one-way discourse; it involves the gaining, holding, and yielding of turns, the negotiation of meaning and direction, the shifting of topic, the signalling and identification of turn type, the use of voice quality, face, and body. Conversation analysis has provided many insights into these features, and should dispel any lingering convictions, left over from the days before the advent of the tape recorder, that conversation is just the same as other discourse types, though perhaps served up faster, with a generous helping of 'idioms'. But the problem is that conversation analysis is an academic study not a pedagogic one, and some of the mechanisms which it reveals, because they happen at speed and are among the features of language which are least accessible to consciousness, are extremely difficult to teach.

10.4 Conversation activities

▶ TASK 66

In a chapter on discussion in her book *Developing Communication Skills*, Pat Pattison lists problems with discussion classes and goes on to suggest a number of activities which may help by focusing upon the content, reason, and result of discussion, as well as on the number of participants. She does, however, reject the idea of giving model phrases, saying: 'No model phrases are suggested for these activities. In my experience, learners feel hampered in expressing their opinions by the need to use prescribed formulae, if they are not ready to use them naturally' (Pattison 1987:244).

Do you agree?

Despite the problems outlined in **10.3** there are, nevertheless, many ways in which the insights of conversation analysis can be exploited in the classroom. Most obviously, the phrases, words, and noises associated with particular turn types, as well as with the getting, holding, and passing of turns may be taught quite explicitly. Thus the following kinds of association between mechanism and realization can be made:

Opening: *Hello there; Hi; How are you?; How's things?*
Taking a turn: *Yes but; Well yes but; Surely . . .*
Holding a turn: *er; um; anyway; you know; I mean; sort of*
Passing a turn: *What do you think?*; tag questions
Closing: *Right; Well anyway; So; OK then*
Pre-sequence: *Listen; Did I tell you about? Oh I wanted to ask you*
Repair
– self: *What I really meant was*
– other: *Sorry; I don't quite get what you mean*
Upshot
– own: *What I'm getting at is*
– other's: *What are you getting at?*

Other means of turn-taking which do not associate with phrases, words, or noises, such as pause or overlap, changes in voice quality, elongation of syllable, pitch rise, and all the signals of body, face, and eyes, are of course not so easily taught, but here there is the possibility of exploiting the cassette or video recorder, either to observe native speaker interaction, or to record students' own conversation and then overtly discuss the success or appropriateness of the strategies employed, as well as reasons for misunderstandings, and differences between the students' culture and that associated with the language they are learning.

▶ TASK 67

The following are transcripts of dialogues. One of these dialogues is invented, one is unscripted but created for teaching, and the other is authentic conversation between native speakers. Can you tell which is which, and if so, how?

Extract A

> R: It's o—it's okay we'll pop down tomorrow Gertrude
> C: You sure you don't, it is an awful lot of it, you want to quickly nip down now for it.
> R: Okay I will. Er *HEY* you hmm that is have you been lighting a fire down there?

(*Levinson 1983:313*)

INTERVIEWER: Ah come in, Ms Wilson. Please take a seat.
TANIA: Thank you.
INTERVIEWER: You'd like to work as a model—is that right?
TANIA: Yes, I would.
INTERVIEWER: OK—first of all, could I have your personal details for our records?
What's your first name?
TANIA: Tania—that's T-A-N-I-A.
INTERVIEWER: So that's Ms Tania Wilson. You're American, I guess?
TANIA: Yes, I am.
INTERVIEWER: And how old are you?
TANIA: I'm twenty.
INTERVIEWER: Uh huh . . . how tall are you?
TANIA: I'm five foot seven.
INTERVIEWER: Hmm—that's not very tall. We like our models to be taller than that—what colour is your hair?
TANIA: Can't you see?
INTERVIEWER: Well, I can see that it's blonde now, but what colour is it really?
TANIA: It really is blonde—it's natural!
INTERVIEWER: Oh, I see. I'm sorry—you've got beautiful hair. And what colour are your eyes?
TANIA: They're blue-grey—it depends on the weather!
INTERVIEWER: All right. Now, Ms Wilson, I can't promise you any work—but I've got your details and if anything comes up, I'll give you a call . . .

(*Garton-Sprenger and Greenall* 1986:83)

BG: Tell me—tell me where you live.
DF: Okay, I live in a flat. . . Okay?
BG: Yes. How many rooms has it got?
DF: Erm, well there's a front room with a kitchen off it, at the back, er, well—you come into the hall first of all, so—then off that you have the front room and the kitchen, a bathroom . . . erm, and a bedroom, at the back.
BG: . . . And have you got a garden?
DF: Yes. Just for me.
BG: That's jolly nice.

(*Willis and Willis* 1988:52b)

1 In what ways might these dialogues make students aware of features of conversation in English?
2 Do authentic or unscripted conversations have any necessary advantage over invented ones in presenting students with these features?
3 To what extent do you think that authentic conversation is likely to be suitable only for advanced students?
4 Do you think students should see the transcripts of conversation materials that are used, and if so, at what point?
5 Is it possible to judge these extracts without hearing them?

Recordings can bring some aspects of native speakers' conversation into the classroom, and transcripts can bring them out of time and on to the page where they can be seen and discussed. Yet whether we use invented, unscripted, or authentic material, there are many important visual aspects of conversation which cannot be captured on cassette or in writing. For those institutions rich enough to have video equipment, the observation of video conversation may provide even better material. It is true that, like tape recording, the act of video recording to some extent destroys an important aspect of conversation, making it for an outside audience rather than private to the participants, yet even such highly public interactions as TV chat shows and interviews preserve many of the features of self-contained conversation, as do those unscripted soap operas and films in which actors improvise with a knowledge of plot. And there are language teaching videos which make use of such material (for example, *BBC Television English* (1985–7) and *Impact* (Revell 1988)).

▶ TASK 68

To what extent can pictures or still photographs substitute for the visual aspects of conversation which are lost on tape or paper? What role do you consider the stills perform in the following presentation of dialogue?

all (of) these letters
all of them

some of the requests
some of them

both (of) these people
both of them

one of his records
one of them

(*Eastwood, Kay, Mackin, and Strevens 1981:63*)

10.5 An approach to conversation development

In their book, *Conversation*, Nolasco and Arthur (1987) suggest dividing activities developing conversation into four types, and give detailed and various activities within each category. The four categories are:

1 *Controlled activities*, including many quite traditional 'closed' activities, in which speech is rigorously limited by instructions, such as:

– the giving and eliciting of personal information by substitution: (*I'm X and I'm from Y; where are you from?*)
– memorizing dialogue and repeating it either along with the original recording or with another student acting as prompter
– caricatured, exaggerated (and therefore humorous) imitation of native speaker sounds and intonation
– information gap activities, sometimes involving movement around the classroom, for example, students are given half of an exchange and have to find the student with the other half

– questions likely to elicit target grammatical structures
– the use of flow diagrams, giving the topic or function of each utterance, but not its realization, for example:

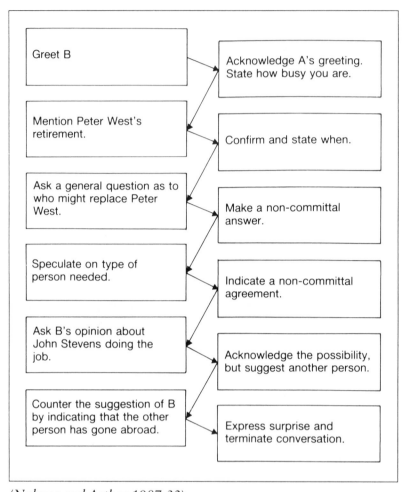

(*Nolasco and Arthur 1987:32*)

2 *Awareness activities*, making extensive use of tape and (where possible) video recordings of native speakers in conversation, such as:

– identifying words and phrases used as turn-taking mechanisms
– watching vision without sound or hearing sound without vision and guessing at the contents of the missing channel.

3 *Fluency activities*, making use of communicative activities such as role play, games, and discussion.

4 *Feedback activities*, in which students, using tape, video, or observation of each other, analyse their own interaction and, for example:

- note the presence or absence of features identified by awareness activities
- note the strategies they have used to achieve certain purposes
- overtly discuss communication problems in the culture of the language they are learning.

▶ TASK 69

1   Which of Nolasco and Arthur's categories are holistic activities, involving students in something approximating to actual conversation, and which are atomistic activities, isolating elements of conversational activity and developing them in readiness for 'the real thing'?

2   Given the speed and interactivity of conversation, its exploitation of every linguistic and paralinguistic resource, and the fact that it is the discourse type in which it is hardest to concentrate on fluency and accuracy at the same time, how valid are atomistic activities in conversation development?

10.6 Conversation and cultural appropriateness

More than any other discourse type, conversation raises the vexed issue of the need and justification for effecting cultural as well as linguistic changes in student behaviour. Whatever the universality of the principles of co-operation and politeness, it is clear that the realization of the politeness principle in communication varies greatly from culture to culture (Brown and Levinson 1978), particularly in interaction whose prime motive is establishing and maintaining social relationships. It is therefore possible to make general statements about the culturally variable implicature of almost any aspect of conversation: of the significance of overlap and interruption, of repetition of offers, of phatic noises during a long turn, of the distance between speakers, of the conversational rights of women and men, or old and young. Instances of such differences are well documented, and well known to any person who has had the enriching experience of social interaction in more than one culture. The problem really is twofold: firstly, any statement about contrastive pragmatics will be open to question and debate; secondly, even if we can identify differences, we may not wish to teach them, and our students may not wish to learn them. Students may feel that a feature of the conversational mechanisms of their own culture—let us say privileges in turn-taking for older people—is intrinsically good, or a part of their cultural identity which they do not wish to yield. Many languages, moreover, and the English language in particular, are native languages in diverse cultures (the Caribbean, North America, Ireland, for example), or may be used as a means of communication in interactions in which none of the participants belongs to an English-speaking culture.

▶ TASK 70

In Russian culture the following appear to be more frequent features of interaction than they are in British culture:

- the absence of a translation equivalent of 'goodbye' at the end of a telephone call
- long uninterrupted turns during casual conversation
- the phatic use of the sound conventionally written as 'uh-huh' or 'mhuh' in English, with a voice quality which in English can indicate boredom
- interruption of a speaker to say that what he or she is saying is already known to the hearer
- asking directly, and without elaborate apology, for small favours: for example, a cigarette, a coin for the telephone
- comment by older people upon the behaviour and dress of younger people
- standing up for elderly people on public transport
- offering food to visitors.

1 Which of these, if any, do you think someone teaching Russian students English should attempt to make them change when they are speaking English?

2 Make a list of similar differences between British culture and one you are familiar with and consider how you would approach them when teaching English.

These are, of course, broad issues on which every student and teacher must make up his or her own mind. It is possible, however, to generalize and categorize, as in Figure 14.

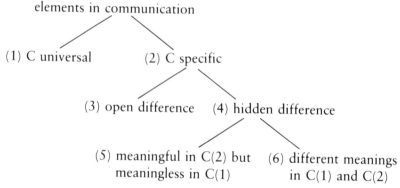

Figure 14 (C = culture)

Figure 14 may be glossed as follows. We may assume that some elements of communication are universal (1) (though these might have to be couched in such very general terms as 'causing physical pain is a sign of unfriendliness'), and that others are culture specific (2). If this is the case, then universal features will cause no problem, only culture-specific ones. Among these, some differences will be immediately evident (3). The Indian salutation with both palms pressed together in front of the forehead is a good example. It is clear that some signal is being sent, but this signal does not mean anything in many other cultures. There are, however, differences which may not be so easily apparent (4). Wearing shoes does not communicate any particular social meaning in British culture, but it may be offensive in certain categories of building in other cultures. A British person may therefore simply not realize that a signal is being sent (5) and there will therefore be a failure of communication. Moreover, there are hidden differences which are not easily realized, and which mean different things in different cultures (6); in which case there is not only a failure of communication, but also communication of something which was not intended, or even—in the worse case—which is the opposite of the intention. A clear example of this category (6) is nodding by someone from a culture where nodding means 'yes' in a culture where it means 'no'. Another example is critical distance (the distance which speakers should preserve between them if they are not to signal aggression or intimacy). It has been said that this is shorter in Arab culture than in North American culture. Yet as the meaning of distance is present in both cultures, then a North American may *wrongly* interpret the Arab speaker as aggressive or over-intimate, and the Arab may interpret the North American as unfriendly or off-hand, without either being aware of the reason. It seems reasonable to suggest, taking account of the respect which all human beings should have for the cultural identity of all others, that the foreign language learner entering another culture, and, *equally importantly*, native speakers in contact with people from other cultures, should be made especially aware of differences in category (6) and certain instances of (5) and (4) as well. The decision on whether to adopt that feature is then their own.

▶ TASK 71

Consider the following extract from an exercise on conversational alternatives:

Doing the Right Thing

How much do you know about the way the British live and behave? Do this quiz.

You're in Britain

1 You're visiting the house of a British friend. It's very beautiful. Do you:
  a) tell him how beautiful it is?
  b) ask how much it cost?
  c) ask if he'll take you round every room?

  (. . .)

4 You meet a British friend in the street. You last saw him two days ago. Do you:
  a) just say hello?
  b) say hello and shake his hand?
  c) put your arm round his shoulder and slap him on the back?

5 You're at a party and have just been introduced to someone. While you are talking he mentions that his wife is not at the party. Do you:
  a) ask where his wife is?
  b) change the subject?
  c) ask if he gets on well with his wife?

(Morrow and Johnson 1979:5)

The other four questions in this exercise describe similar alternatives. Each answer has a score. Top scores for the questions here are for 1(a), 4(a), 5(b).

1 Do you think it is possible to generalize about behaviour within a culture in the way that this exercise implies?

2 If so, do you think the scoring for these questions gives an accurate picture of British life?

3 What, in general, do you think of the approach in this exercise?

▶ TASK 72

A student is learning British English in order to do business with other foreign speakers of English. The culture of the student and of his or her potential contacts have elements of conversational management in common with each other which are not shared by British culture. Do you think you should teach the student to abandon these in favour of more British behaviour?

11   Focusing on cohesion

11.1 Introduction

The lowest level of Figure 8 (in 7.2) which falls within the domain of discourse is cohesion. This is an area which is of relevance to all discourse, spoken and written, 'one-way' and 'two-way' alike, although the choice of appropriate cohesive ties is profoundly affected by whether the discourse is spoken or written, and by the discourse type.

Cohesion has often been neglected in language teaching, where sentences have been created, manipulated, and assessed in isolation. It has been assumed that student difficulties arise primarily from lack of vocabulary or the complexity of grammatical structure at sentence level, whereas difficulties can as easily arise from problems with cohesion: finding the referent for a pronoun, for example, or recovering a phrase or clause lost through ellipsis.

The results of this neglect are familiar to teachers and learners at all levels, for they affect both production and processing. In production they can result in the creation of a stretch of language in which every sentence, in isolation, is faultless, yet the overall effect is one of incoherence or inappropriateness. In processing they manifest themselves in a sensation known to all language learners: that of understanding every word and every construction in each individual sentence, but still not understanding the whole.

The neglect of cohesion arises partly from a simple lack of awareness. Although grammar has been extensively studied, Anglo-American linguistics in the middle decades of this century, believing the sentence to be the highest unit amenable to formal analysis, paid little attention to cohesion (see 1.5–1.6). The current revival of interest dates only from the mid 1970s and, in particular, from the publication of Halliday and Hasan's *Cohesion in English* in 1976. Where there has been knowledge of cohesion in language teaching, there has sometimes been an implicit assumption that cohesive links must operate between sentences in the same way in the first and second language, in other words, through straightforward translation equivalents. Even now, when extensive research has been done on cohesion, there is still a reluctance to give it much prominence in language pedagogy. In part this stems from a bottom-up approach. Cohesion between sentences is too easily seen as an aspect of language use to be developed after the ability to handle grammar and words within sentences.

In addition, the situation is made worse by the traditional approach which prefers a use to be right or wrong. The cohesion *between* sentences is not as easily assessed as the grammar *within* them. It is often a matter of style, different uses being appropriate to particular discourse types (see Cook 1989). This role of cohesion in creating style is yet another reason for its neglect, for style is often considered to be the concern of advanced students only. This belief is unfortunate, for an error of style can so antagonize an interlocutor that it will negate the positive effects of lower level accuracy. Style should be a major concern of all students.

▶ TASK 73

Christine Nuttall suggests that cohesion may be tackled by identifying problems and then asking questions in which the meaning of the cohesive item is made explicit. For example, the clause 'The Greeks believed so' would give rise to the question: 'What did the Greeks believe?' She goes on to say:

The answers to these questions have to be found by searching the text and using your common sense and knowledge of the context. (. . .) To develop this skill does not require complicated exercises; it is sufficient to ask questions of the kind given above. The difficulty is to make students realize the value of this activity and to prevent them from dismissing it as trivial. You cannot prepare exercises precisely for this purpose, since the point is lost unless each example is located in an extended text. The best way is therefore to make use of every opportunity to draw attention to these features in the texts for other purposes.
(*Nuttall 1982: 91*)

Do you agree with her that
– common sense and knowledge of context is enough to interpret cohesion?
– students are likely to dismiss exercises on cohesion as trivial?
– study of cohesion is best mixed with other aspects of discourse?

11.2 Activities developing cohesion

Activities focusing on cohesion will need to consider every intersection on the grid in Figure 15. They should, however, avoid confusing the *use of* cohesion with *knowledge about* cohesion. There is no need to burden students with the cumbersome terminology for analysing cohesion used in linguistics. As teachers we will need to approach any stretch of language in two ways. We need first to analyse its cohesive devices and their stylistic effect, and secondly to devise activities which will develop their use and understanding by the student. But the two stages should not be confused.

	Processing	Production
Verb form		
Reference		
Repetition		
Lexical chains		
Substitution		
Ellipsis		
Conjunction		

(Parallelism is omitted here, on the grounds that it is used less frequently; the ordering of information in the clause is also in part a cohesive device, but has been dealt with as an aspect of shared knowledge in **8.3**.)

Figure 15

We shall look at an example, chosen for its density of cohesive devices, first analyse its cohesion, and then consider ways in which it might be presented to students. The passage is from a play. It is not therefore real speech, but it has incorporated some of its features. It illustrates the fact that texts which are lexically and grammatically quite simple at sentence level can be very complicated—and therefore confusing—in their cohesion. Notice, however, that although the passage is an extract from a longer discourse, all the cohesive devices can be interpreted without reference to earlier or later parts of the whole text. If there had been cohesive devices referring to other parts of the text, they would need some explanation. This point is often overlooked in the presentation of extracts for language teaching (Cook 1986a).

The passage is as follows:

'What's it matter? You start a family, work and plan. Suddenly you turn around and there's nothing there. Probably never was. What's a family, anyway? Just—just kids with your blood in 'em. There's no reason why they should like you. You go on expecting it, of course, but it's silly, really. Like expecting 'em to know what they mean to you when they're babies. They're not supposed to know perhaps. It's not natural really, when you come to think of it. You can't expect anybody to know what they mean to somebody else—it's not the way of things. There's just nothing. Bloody nothing.'
(Peter Shaffer: *Five Finger Exercise*)

From a vocabulary point of view this is quite elementary. Although there are some very colloquial uses (*kids* meaning *children*, *bloody* for emphasis, and *things* meaning *life in general*), the majority of words could be expected to occur quite early in a learner's vocabulary. From a grammatical point of view the passage is also quite simple. The finite verbs, with only one exception, are in the present or the simple past. Only six of the fourteen orthographic sentences have subordinate clauses, and most of these are in end position.

In the use of cohesive devices, however, the passage is rich and complex. We can show this by underlining each referring expression and inserting the symbol Ø for each elliptic word. There are only three co-ordinating conjunctions in this passage but there are phatic 'filler' expressions which also serve a cohesive purpose and we can place brackets around both categories. Our analysis will now yield:

'What's <u>it</u> matter? <u>You</u> start a family, Ø work (and) Ø plan. Suddenly <u>you</u> turn around (and) there's nothing <u>there</u>. Probably Ø never was Ø Ø. What's a family, (anyway)? Ø Ø Just—just kids with <u>your</u> blood in 'em. There's no reason why <u>they</u> should like <u>you</u>. <u>You</u> go on expecting <u>it</u>, (of course), (but) <u>it's</u> silly, (really). Ø Ø Like expecting 'em to know what <u>they</u> mean to <u>you</u> when <u>they're</u> babies. <u>They're</u> not supposed to know Ø Ø Ø Ø Ø Ø Ø Ø Ø perhaps. <u>It's</u> not natural (really), [when <u>you</u> come to think of <u>it</u>]. <u>You</u> can't expect <u>anybody</u> to know what <u>they</u> mean to somebody else—<u>it's</u> not the way of things. There's just nothing. Bloody nothing.'

The problem is how we can exploit this type of analysis to develop both an understanding of these cohesive devices and the ability to use them appropriately, but without burdening students with linguistic terminology. Our answers to the problem will depend upon whether we are concentrating on processing or production, and it will not often be practical to use the same passage for both at once. Concentrating upon processing, we might ask simply:

1 Give the meaning of the underlined words.
2 The symbol Ø shows that the speaker has left out a word or phrase. What words or phrases are they?

These are straightforward comprehension questions, rather like the traditional ones which test vocabulary. They can be phrased as they are here, or presented with multiple-choice alternatives, exploiting the absurdity of misinterpreted reference. If we wish them to be answered as the text is being processed, rather than retrospectively, then they can be included in the text or printed alongside it.

Concentrating upon the production of cohesive devices, we might first substitute the full form for referring expressions whose meaning has to be recovered from outside the sentence. (Referring expressions which refer to another word or phrase within the same sentence are best left.) Our passage would now read:

'What does life matter? A person starts a family, works and plans. Suddenly the person turns around and there's nothing in life. Probably never was. What's a family, anyway? Just—just kids with a person's blood in them. There's no reason why the kids should like the person. The person goes on expecting the kids to like him or her, of course, but the situation is silly, really. Like expecting the kids to know what they mean to their parent when they are babies. The kids are not supposed to know perhaps. Children knowing what they mean to their parents is not natural really, when you come to think of it. A person can't expect another person to know what they mean to somebody else—knowing what one person means to another is not the way of things. There's just nothing. Bloody nothing.'

and an exercise on it could read:

— Substitute the following for words in the passage, but without changing the meaning. Use each word once only. Make any other changes which are necessary.

> you   you   you   your   it   it   they   they   anybody
> you   you   you   it   it   it   they   there   them

In this form, this exercise is very difficult. It can be made easier, and thus adjusted to the level of particular students, by changing only some of the referring items, and leaving others in their original form. As it is here, however, the exercise will reveal two common problems for even quite advanced learners: the use of *you* as a general pronoun meaning *one/a person* and the very complex reference of *it*, which in this short passage refers to a concept not mentioned explicitly (*life* or *the situation in general*), as well as to clauses derived from, but not the same as, a clause in a previous sentence (*them to like you / expecting them to like you / their knowing what they mean to you when they're babies / people knowing what they mean to somebody else*). *It* may also, very confusingly, sometimes function as what grammarians call a *dummy* subject. This is possibly the case in the sentence *It's silly, really* which could be interpreted as: either *it is silly expecting them to like you* in which *it* is a dummy and *expecting them to like you* is omitted through ellipsis; or as *expecting them to like you is silly*, in which case *it = expecting them to like you*. Such complicated reference is unlikely to be uncovered simply by 'common sense and knowledge of the context'.

Still concentrating upon production, we might now write in all the words omitted through ellipsis. (To avoid confusion in the following exercise, it is also necessary to omit the fillers and conjunctions.) The passage would now read:

'What's it matter? You start a family, you work, you plan. Suddenly you turn around. There's nothing there. Probably there never was anything there. What's a family? It is just kids with your blood in 'em. There's no reason why they should like you. You go on expecting it. It's silly. It is like expecting 'em to know what they mean to you when they're babies. They're not supposed to know what they mean to you when they are babies perhaps. It's not natural. You can't expect anybody to know what they mean to somebody else—it's not the way of things. There's just nothing. Bloody nothing.'

The students may now be asked:

– Without changing the meaning, take out at least eighteen words.

But we should not be too dogmatic about their answers. They may well find other words which can validly be omitted.

Although there are so few instances of conjunction, or perhaps *because* there are so few, it is quite easy to devise exercises which practise conjunction as well. The instruction, for example, could be:

– Insert the following words into the passage: *nevertheless, because, however, then, yet, therefore, and.*

▶ TASK 74

Nuttall suggests the following methods of demonstrating cohesion:

(a) More advanced students may enjoy making their own questions, searching the text for items they think may baffle their colleagues. This gives good practice in focusing their attention on potential problems, a skill they need for tackling texts independently.

(b) *Supply* a suitable text (. . .) Put boxes round suitable items.
Task: Students find all other items with the same reference as each boxed item; they circle each one and join them with lines to the appropriate boxed items.
Or use different colours: all items with the same referent will be underlined or circled with the same colour. *Note* This kind of activity is best demonstrated by working through a text on the OHP (. . .)

(c) *Supply* a text with the reference items (or some of them) omitted and replaced by gaps. Supply also a list of the omitted items in random order.

How successful would you expect these strategies to be? How well would they work with the passage we have analysed? Are there aspects of cohesion to which they do not draw attention?

▶ TASK 75

Look back at the approximation exercise in **9.6** based on a passage about birds. There we considered approximation as a means of drawing students' attention to the functional organization within a discourse part. Now consider the same exercise as a means of developing cohesion in discourse production. Which aspects of cohesion on the grid in Figure 15 would be practised?

11.3 Conclusion

The exercises discussed in **11** may seem rather dry, and reminiscent—with their gaps to be filled and requests for alternative words—of the grammar exercises and comprehension questions of traditional language teaching books. The comparisons are justified, for like their traditional counterparts these activities are atomistic, and they isolate an aspect of the language system, and concentrate upon it. Yet as with any atomistic activity, there is nothing inherently bad in this isolation, provided it remains in a subordinate relationship to more holistic activities, and does not become an end in itself. We need always to remember that the final goal of the language student is to operate the interlocking systems of discourse, vocabulary, grammar, and pronunciation in their entirety. It is to activities which involve everything at once that we shall turn our attention next.

12 General discourse activities

12.1 Introduction

Activities concerning the 'top' levels of discourse are inherently holistic. Hypotheses about interlocutors, orientation towards discourse type and part, and conceptions of discourse function necessarily subsume the 'lower' levels of discourse like cohesion, as well as formal levels of language: grammar, vocabulary, and pronunciation. Nevertheless, the activities we have examined so far in **8–11** have focused upon particular aspects of discourse processing and production, rather than general practice.

We need now to consider activities which can develop discourse skills, without concentration on any one aspect in isolation. These will be activities in which students handle all the interlocking systems of discourse at once, and those of grammar, vocabulary, and pronunciation as well. That is, after all, what students must do when they communicate in the world outside the classroom. The problem is to develop such activities within the specific environment of the institutional classroom, with its very limited and idiosyncratic social framework, in which, traditionally, the student enters into only two kinds of relationship: passive subordination to the teacher, and egalitarian camaraderie with fellow students. If we wish our students to become competent in discourse, we will need to involve them in communication with a variety of interlocutors in different relationships to them, through a variety of discourse types, with a variety of functions, in both speech and writing and process and production, to deal with the interaction of these elements in discourse, in different combinations—and with rapid changes too.

The communicative approach has designed many such activities, because using language for communication of necessity involves discourse in operation. Yet despite the prolific theoretical writings in support of a communicative approach, and its widespread acceptance, many students and teachers, examiners and syllabus writers, still feel that the real stuff of language development must reside in more tedious and laborious atomistic study. Activities in which students handle discourse most fully are considered to be in some way marginal: entertainments to fill a few minutes at the end of a lesson.

Atomistic activities are more easily examined and graded, and the pressure on many students and teachers of language to substitute the goal of examination success for that of communicative competence is perhaps another reason for their elevation. Yet the preparation of students for examination and grading can become antithetical to language development. Although atomistic activities most certainly have an important function, they are of little benefit if they cannot be reassimilated into the whole, to help students in the handling of discourse in communication.

12.2 General activities: an example

With the need for general discourse practice in mind, it is as well to examine any language teaching activity for the practice it provides in the elements of discourse, so that students may have varied practice, either within one activity or over a range of them. We shall assess one activity in this way, as an example. It comes from *Towards the Creative Teaching of English* (Melville, Langenheim, Rinvolucri, and Spaventa 1980) and draws on an exercise which is a staple of communicative language teaching, and which we have already mentioned (**9.6**) for its role in sensitizing students to discourse structure: the re-ordering of jumbled sentences. This is by now a fairly commonplace pedagogic activity, though this fact in itself should count neither for nor against it. This task, however, involves more than simple rearrangement.

The procedure is as follows. Each student is given a piece of paper on which is written one sentence of the following story.

There were four people sitting in a train in Vietnam in the late sixties.

The four people were as follows: a young Vietnamese who loved his country, an old Vietnamese grandmother, a beautiful young girl of about eighteen, and an ugly American soldier.

Suddenly the train went into a tunnel.

There was the sound of a kiss.

All four people heard a slap.

When the train came out of the tunnel, the Vietnamese could see that the G.I.'s face was red.

The beautiful young girl glanced at the granny and the soldier in astonishment.

The granny was asleep in the corner of the compartment.

The young patriot grinned happily.

The problem is: who kissed who and who slapped who?

(*Melville, Langenheim, Rinvolucri, and Spaventa 1980:85*)

By talking together, they must decide on the original order, and solve the problem. As in other recombination activities in the book, the following rules must be obeyed:

- You can read your paper out to the group, but you *must not show* it to anyone.
- Don't write.
- Only ask me, the teacher, language questions.

The teacher is recommended to avoid intervention in the task by, for example, pre-teaching vocabulary, sitting outside the group, avoiding eye-contact, only intervening if absolutely necessary and then only by writing on the blackboard.

▶ TASK 76

Assess the advantages and disadvantages of the activity described above. Are there, for example, any practical problems, and if so, could they be overcome? Is the activity more suitable for certain categories of student than for others? Does the fact that there are ten sentences mean that it can only be used in classes with ten (or multiples of ten) students?

What linguistic and discoursal skills does the activity involve? Which of these are generated by the teacher's non-participation and the co-operative nature of the enterprise?

This apparently simple activity is both motivating and entertaining, for puzzles and problems of this kind have an intrinsic interest, even for native speakers, and are widely popular. It also involves students in a wide range of discoursal activity, involving both spoken and written language, production and processing, and several discourse types: negotiation, conversation, narrative, and riddle. If the rules are followed, the activity will involve students in all of the following discourse and language skills:

- negotiation of relationships and roles within the group
- discussion of procedure
- turn-taking without control by the teacher
- application of schemata: about trains, tunnels, the Vietnam war, likely sequences of events in narrative and riddles (kiss then slap)
- knowledge of narrative structure: i.e. initial situation, event, new situation
- article use indicating previous mention or assumed default in schema
- reading aloud with accurate enough pronunciation to be understood
- the handling and repetition of new vocabulary in context
- repetition of correct sentences
- following lexical chains (four people . . . grandmother . . . granny / American soldier . . . G.I. . . . the soldier / a young Vietnamese who loved his country . . . the patriot)
- problem solving (the best answer is that the patriot kissed his own hand and then slapped the soldier)
- assessing hypotheses

- arguing a point of view
- reaching a consensus as a group
- presentation of a group decision to an outsider (the teacher)
- reading a story aloud.

It may also involve:
- regulation of relationships within the group: urging another student to participate; curbing a domineering student
- conflict and argument with other students
- dispute with the teacher (some students will not accept the teacher's inactivity)
- discussion of wider issues raised by the story: for example, politics, sexual stereotypes, lateral thinking, the role of the teacher.

One of the reasons that this activity generates such a wide range of practice is its restructuring of the traditional lines of communication in the classroom between teacher (T) and students (S) (Figure 16). This gives the student both a wider range of relationships, and conversational autonomy, bringing a corresponding variety of discourse.

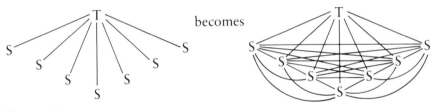

Figure 16

▶ TASK 77

Although the withdrawal of the teacher during this activity may generate a greater variety of discourse, it may also have the disadvantage of depriving the students of a linguistic example and instruction. Do you feel that this is the case? What provision would you make for this?

The least desirable approach to this activity is perhaps to predict difficulties and explain them beforehand, as this disrupts one of the advantages of this kind of activity: that language knowledge is sought only when necessary for language use. To answer questions when requested runs the gauntlet of re-involving the teacher. So perhaps the best solution, when no student knows and guesses fail, is to allow students to do what they would do in authentic communication when no one around them knows an important word: use a dictionary! The teacher may also point out and discuss pronunciation, grammatical and discoursal problems which arose in the activity—*after* it is finished.

▶ TASK 78

If the temporary withdrawal of the teacher's direction and the co-operative enterprise of the students increase the range of discoursal skills being practised, to what degree is the same true of pairwork? Consider the following conflicting recommendations from two English courses for young learners (five- to eleven-year-olds).

Some of the activities use pairwork. But because some teachers do not like pairwork, or have too many pupils in the class to make it possible, an alternative to pairwork is always given.
(*Johnson 1983:7*)

. . . pair work is invaluable in maximizing the involvement of all pupils. Individual capabilities vary but even less able pupils will be more active and involved in their own learning than if the teacher is asking all the questions. Initially pair work may be time consuming but a little initial patience in using the above techniques will be greatly rewarded.
(*Ashworth and Clark 1989:3*)

Which do you agree with, and why?

12.3 Conclusion

The activity which we described in **12.2**, though it may not have been designed with discourse in mind, has been chosen here as an example of an enjoyable and motivating activity which generates a wide range of discoursal practice. When choosing activities from existing materials, it can only be to the good to assess the practice which they offer in the various elements structuring discourse, ensuring that students, in the course of their studies, experience a variety of senders and receivers, social relationships, schemata, discourse types, topics, and functions, as well as gaining practice in orientating themselves within the internal structure of discourses, and with conversational mechanisms and cohesion. Only by exposure to a wide selection of these elements, interacting in a multitude of ways, can students become fully competent users of the language they are learning.

Exploration
Discourse development in the classroom

In this section the focus is on ways in which teachers can explore and make use of the theoretical and pedagogic approaches to discourse described in Sections One and Two. We shall carry out this exploration through a series of tasks, suggesting practical activities and exercises. The order of topics will be very close to that of Section Two, dealing with the most general aspects of discourse first. Where passages are given, these should be treated as examples only. If you feel any passage is unsuitable, analyse why this is so, and try to find one which is better suited to the level and interests of your own students.

▶ TASK 79

Aim
To examine the approach to discourse in the materials you use and to consider adapting it if necessary. (This very general aim should be carried out by working through the tasks which follow.)

Resources
The textbooks, syllabus, or materials you use.

Procedure
As you work through the tasks in this section, assess whether your materials attempt to classify discourse in any principled way: for example, by discourse type, topic, function, or situation. Is discourse approached top-down or bottom-up, atomistically or holistically? If there are atomistic activities, what areas of language or discourse do they focus on? Do they attempt to reintegrate these areas?

Evaluation
How successful do you consider the approach in your materials to be? Consider how it might be improved, either by adaptation, addition, or rearrangement of material.

▶ TASK 80

Aim
To implement a top-down approach to comprehension. To decide what kind of information students need before they can make sense of difficult

discourse. To devise and implement questions guiding students to understanding through higher level information.

Resources
Figure 8 (in **7.2**), as a guide to levels of information. Your answer to Task 40. The following piece of transcribed speech (or a passage of your own).

'Do you see intellectuals have the problem of having to have to understand it and then listen to it. They can't feel anything. So that's their problem. So the only way to get to an intellectual is to talk to him and then play him the record. You couldn't put the record on and then let him hear it. So the guy in *The Times* whoever he was who wrote that thing about Mailer's fingers or whatever the hell he wrote you know was *Pseud's Corner* you know. But it worked and we were flattered.'

Procedure
Note the points of difficulty in a first reading. Then read the passage again in the light of the following information (some of which you may have guessed or know already).

1 The speaker is the Beatle John Lennon. He is answering a question during a radio interview (broadcast in *The Words and Music of John Lennon*, BBC Radio 1, 1985).

2 The prestigious British newspaper *The Times* compared a Beatles record to a passage in a novel by Norman Mailer.

3 *Pseud's Corner* is a column quoting pieces of pretentious writing in the British satirical magazine *Private Eye*.

Consider how this *high-level* information about sender, receiver, and discourse type affects lower levels like turn-taking and cohesion, and the assumptions the speaker is making about the receivers. Using Task 40 as a model, devise and implement questions on this high-level information.

Evaluation
1 What effect did the questions about higher levels of discourse have on your students' understanding? If possible, try out the same passage on two different groups, in one case providing questions on higher levels, and in the other only questions on lower levels. Then compare the comprehension of the two groups.

2 Consider what types of discourse are most likely to pose problems of the same kind as the one above. How may hearing spoken discourse provide clues to high-level information?

▶ TASK 81

Aim
To devise and implement a top-down approach to passages in which unknown vocabulary poses processing problems.

Resources
Figure 8, as a guide to levels of information. Your answer to Task 40. A passage which poses the same kind of vocabulary problems for your students as the following will for a non-specialist native speaker.

Open the hood and free the contact block and rubber cap behind the headlight. Twist the bayonet grip to the left and pull out the bulb holder. Exchange the faulty bulb, being careful to avoid touching the glass with the fingers. Reassemble, making sure the guide lug is properly seated and the bayonet ring engages the three studs. Fit the rubber cap carefully, so that it fits snugly round the holder with the drain hole lowermost.
(*Saab 96 Maintenance Manual*)

Procedure
1 Consider what general features you would need to establish about the passage before tackling the vocabulary.
2 Devise questions checking that students are starting out with knowledge of these features, and try them out.

Evaluation
1 When faced with a passage, do students tend to believe that unknown vocabulary is the only block to understanding? In this example—or the one you have chosen—how may higher-level knowledge help in understanding individual words?
2 How would a native speaker ascertain the meaning of unknown words?

▶ **TASK 82**

Aim
To consider the effect of social relationships on the development of your students' discourse skills.

Resources
Your knowledge of individual students. Classroom observation. Discussion in **8.2**.

Procedure
1 Consider the degree to which being a teacher or a student may be described in terms of 'status', 'office', and 'role', and how this affects discourse in your classroom. What are the differences between the office, status, and role of individuals in the classroom and out of it? What problems might this cause when they interact in English with people outside the classroom?
2 Think of ways of changing the social structure of your classroom to give students a wider variety of practice. Can you, for example, give students power to initiate or terminate activities, nominate in turn-taking, correct each other, and so on? Try out your ideas.

Evaluation
Are there ways of overcoming the lack of variety in social relationships in your classroom or is it unavoidable in an institutional educational environment? What is the main source of opposition to your innovations?

▶ TASK 83

Aim
To devise and implement activities making students aware of the role of shared knowledge in discourse.

Resources
The discussion in 5 and 8.4 to 8.7. The following extract from a biographical sketch of the gypsy jazz guitarist Django Reinhardt, or a passage of your own choice.

'On January 23rd 1910, a boy was born to a family of nomadic gypsies camped in a field outside the village of Liberchies in Belgium. By the time of his death, 42 years later, that boy, Jean Reinhardt, had become world famous as "Django", the greatest of jazz guitarists, loved and respected by musicians and music lovers of all ages and all tastes.

Many of his compositions have been written down and published, but he did not himself read or write music, and he only learnt to read and write French in his thirties. Yet the amazing flow of his melodies has been captured for all time on many hundreds of recordings.'

(Adapted from sleeve notes by Ken Sykora on the Ace of Clubs record *Django Reinhardt and Stephane Grappelli with The Quintet of the Hot Club of France*)

Procedure
1 Referring back to 8.4 to 8.7, devise exercises on:
   - the quantity of information necessary for a specified receiver
   - article choice for a specified receiver
   - information structure.

2 Decide on ways of introducing these exercises to the students and explaining to them what to do. Then try them out.

Evaluation
1 Note down student reactions and any problems you encounter. In the light of this, make any changes to the exercises which you feel are necessary.

2 You probably spent quite a long time in explanation. Do you feel the activities justify this? Try a similar exercise again at a later date, and compare the success of the second time with the first.

▶ TASK 84

Aim

To explore the relationship between dialogue and monologue, and to use this approach to help students in producing coherent discourse.

Resources

Discussion in **8.8**. The passage you used in Task 83 and another of your own.

Procedure

1 Devise instructions asking students to convert the passage to dialogue.

2 Choose another passage of one-way discourse, write a dialogue from it yourself and give students an instruction to convert this dialogue to monologue.

If you wish you can 'dress up' these rather dry instructions by inventing a situation in which dialogues do become monologues and vice versa. For example, a job application may be realized as a job interview.

Evaluation

1 Note down student reactions to this activity and any problems you encounter. Revise the activity in the light of this and try it out again, if possible on another group.

2 Does all monologic discourse lend itself easily to this exercise? If not, can you characterize the kinds of passages which do? Which is most helpful to students: the conversion of dialogue to monologue or vice versa?

▶ TASK 85

Aim

To explore the problems students may be having with discourse type recognition, and the obstacles this may pose for comprehension.

Resources

The following passages. The discussion in **9**.

1 It is dangerous and an offence to interfere with this apparatus.

2 Could it be their cute, rounded little bodies? Their endearing clumsiness? Their good-humoured smile? Or is that we all remember a comrade, comforter and confidant in the shape of our own childhood teddy?

Ever since President Theodore Roosevelt gave his name to the first *Teddy* bear, people all over the world have fallen in love with these cuddly little creatures. Numerous bears have appeared as heroes of books; they have been immortalised in poetry.

English artist Pam Storey has skilfully captured the lovable attitudes of their tubby bodies and the good-natured expressions of their bear faces in twenty delightful designs. And her designs have been brilliantly translated into bone china figurines by highly skilled craftsmen.

Fine bone china has always been prized for its versatility and capacity to retain fine detail. These assets are amply demonstrated in this very appealing collection. Every figurine not only brings a smile to your lips—you will also be impressed by how skilfully they have been made and painted.

3 GLASS. FRAGILE.

4 To determine the total pension payable, each Community country under whose scheme you have been insured first calculates the amount payable exclusively under its own scheme. Each Community country then calculates what would be payable had the total insurance of each Community country been under its own scheme and then reduces this amount in proportion to the actual periods of insurance under its own scheme in relation to the total insurance periods. You can then receive from each country whichever of the two rates is the most favourable.

5 Sorry for the delay. Ministry of Transport.

6 Faith can move mountains—she's a big girl.

7 He lay flat on the brown, pine needle floor of the forest, his chin on his folded arms, and high overhead the wind blew in the tops of the pine trees.

Procedure
1 Identify the discourse types, and reflect on how you reached your own decisions. Now show your students the passages and ask them to do the same. If they have difficulty, you might wish to focus their attention with questions relating to the features listed in 9.3.

2 For each instance above, consider the effect of depriving it of its physical form and/or situation. (1 appeared on an electric meter; 2 on a glossy leaflet with a credit card bill; 3 on a cardboard box; 4 in an official leaflet about National Insurance; 5 on a motorway road sign; 6 on a lavatory door in two different handwritings; 7 on the first page of a book (*For Whom the Bell Tolls*).)

3 Note that students do not have to understand a passage completely in order to identify its type, and also that they may recognize the type but not know the English word for it.

Evaluation
1 What problems did your students encounter in identifying the discourse types?

2 How culture specific do you think these examples of types are?

3 Do your students know the names of discourse types in English?

▶ TASK 86

Aim

To explore the role of titles in discourse comprehension.

Resources

Textbooks or materials which you use. Your answer to Task 55.

Procedure

1 Do your materials give titles to passages or do they ask students to supply their own? If there are titles, are they informative about content and/or discourse type, or do they serve only to attract attention?

2 Choose a passage and, if possible, use it with two different classes: in one case supplying an informative title, in the other asking students to invent their own.

Evaluation

How important did the title prove to comprehension and orientation? Which is most helpful to discourse development: supplying a title or leaving it out?

▶ TASK 87

Aim

To explore how knowledge of the internal structure of a discourse may help or hinder your students in discourse comprehension.

Resources

A newspaper in English with which you are familiar. Newspaper(s) in the language(s) of your students. The discussion of rank structure in **4.2**.

Procedure

1 Draw a tree diagram of the structure of the newspaper in English. (It may, for example, be divided into Foreign News, Home News, Sports News, etc., and each of these sections may be subdivided.)

2 If possible, compare this structure with that of the foreign language newspaper(s). (If you do not read the language you can ask the student(s) to explain the structure to you.)

3 Devise and implement an exercise helping students to find their way around inside a newspaper. (This need not involve reading and understanding articles in detail.)

4 Devise similar activities for other discourse types: for example, instruction manuals, shopping catalogues, travel guides, TV programmes.

Evaluation

What kind of problems did the structure of the newspaper in English pose for your students? With what discourse types do you think they need most help?

► TASK 88

Aim
To explore the role of the identification of discourse parts.

Resources
A passage from a textbook or reader with which you are familiar. The discussion in **9.4**, especially the extracts from O'Brien and Jordan, Moore *et al.*, and Morrow.

Procedure
1 See whether the parts of the passage are overtly labelled. If not, consider how it might be divided and labelled, and devise and implement an exercise asking students to do this themselves.

2 If parts already have labels, try out the effect of removing them and asking students to replace them.

3 If possible, compare the comprehension of a class who have parts labelled for them with that of one which provides its own.

Evaluation
1 To what degree do you think labelling of parts helps students orientate towards the structure of the passage?

2 Is it best to ask students to supply these labels themselves as a test of comprehension?

3 How might a diagram be used to clarify the relationship of one part to another?

► TASK 89

Aim
To explore the internal structure of a discourse part and to lead students to produce a part with the same structure.

Resources
The passage you used in Task 88. The discussion in **9.4** and **9.5**, and the extracts from Morrow; Grewer, Moston, and Sexton; and Laird.

Procedure
1 Try to divide any of the parts you have identified, whether labelled or not, into functional units. To what extent do these functional units coincide with physical paragraphs or sentences?

2 Indicate the relationship of functional units by means of a diagram. Devise an exercise in which students, using the diagram, produce their own discourse with different information but the same internal structure.

Evaluation
1 Do all discourse types and parts lend themselves as well to representation in diagrams?

2 The exercise here is essentially atomistic. What follow-up activities could reintegrate the awareness of internal structure developed here into more holistic discourse activities?

▶ # TASK 90

Aim
To write instructions for and implement a recombination exercise.

Resources
The following paragraph from a comprehension passage reproduced in the book *Inside Meaning* by Michael Swan.

'Another cause of aggression closely allied to possessiveness is the tendency for children and apes greatly to resent the intrusion of a stranger into their group. A new child in the class may be laughed at, isolated and disliked and even set upon and pinched and bullied. A new monkey may be poked and bitten to death. It is interesting to note that it is only strangeness within a similarity of species that is resented. Monkeys do not mind being joined by a goat or a rat. Children do not object when animals are introduced to the group. Indeed, such novelties are often welcomed. But when monkeys meet a new monkey or children a strange child, aggression often occurs. This suggests strongly that the reason for the aggression is fundamentally possessiveness. The competition of the newcomers is feared.'
(Durbin and Bowlby: *War and Democracy* (quoted in Swan 1975:82))

Procedure
Mix up the sentences and devise instructions for a recombination exercise. Try it out on your students.

Evaluation
1 Are there several ways of recombining the sentences or only one? If there are several ways, what factors does the choice depend on?
2 How would the provision of a title affect the ordering?
3 Should students do this exercise individually, in pairs, in groups, or as a class?

▶ # TASK 91

Aim
To devise and implement an approximation exercise.

Resources
The following passage. The discussion in **9.6**.

The Open University was founded by Royal Charter in 1969, with the aim of providing educational opportunities for adults who wish to study in their own homes and in their own time. Its multi-media approach to teaching—including the use of television broadcasts, correspondence texts, video and audio cassettes as well as face-to-face tuition—has been judged one of the most important innovations ever in the British educational system. It is nationwide, based on thirteen Regional Centres, which provide the necessary local support of information, advice, counselling and tuition. (Open University: *Open Opportunities Guide 1987*)

Procedure
Break down the passage into elementary sentences and write instructions asking students to convey the same information using different discourse types, in different contexts, and with different functions.

Evaluation
What difficulties do students experience? Do you feel it is necessary to incorporate some intermediate stage between the elementary sentences and the final realization: indicating, for example, which elementary sentences should combine into one?

▶ **TASK 92**

Aim
To devise and implement a transfer exercise.

Resources
The discussion in **9.6**. The following invented extract from a curriculum vitae:

1979–83	BA Hons. in English and Spanish at University of Leeds (Class 2.i), including one year (1981–1982) as *au pair* in Segovia, Spain
1983–4	EFL teacher, Casa Inglès, Madrid
1984–5	Part-time Spanish teacher, Fulham Adult Education Institute, London. Private EFL lessons
1985–6	Postgraduate Teaching Certificate specializing in English (mother-tongue) at University of Bristol
1986–8	English Teacher, Bramcote Comprehensive, Nottingham
1988–	Computer Operator Trainee, Plessey, Nottingham

Procedure
Devise and implement instructions for a transfer exercise asking students to convert the information above to:
– an informal letter
– a casual conversation
– an interview for a job
– a formal letter
– an obituary
– a TV programme.

In each instance, you will need to give considerable detail about the receiver (see **8.1**).

Evaluation
Are any atomistic activities necessary as preparation for this exercise?

▶ TASK 93

Aim
To assess whether recombination and approximation are suited to beginners as well as intermediate and advanced students.

Resources
The following passage:

My name's Alice. I've got a sister (her name's Ann), and two brothers, Joe and Philip. We've all got fair hair and blue eyes, and we're all slim except Joe—he's very fat. Ann's very pretty and she's got lots of boyfriends. I've only got one boyfriend: his name's Kevin, and he's very nice.
(*Swan and Walter 1984:44*)

Procedure
Devise a recombination exercise (as in Task 90) and an approximation exercise (as in Task 91) based on this passage. Try it out on students of a suitable level.

Evaluation
Compare your experience in devising an exercise on this passage with that of Tasks 90 and 91. Compare the students' performance. Are there any significant differences?

▶ TASK 94

Aim
To analyse turn-taking in your (or another teacher's) classes.

Resources
A cassette recorder. The transcription conventions in (2) in Task 17; the transcription in Task 24.

Procedure
Record a conversation between students and teacher in the classroom. Transcribe a short portion of it, using the transcription conventions. Pay particular attention to the way turns are gained, held, or passed.

Evaluation
Does the teacher exercise turn-taking rights beyond those of the students? Does the teacher nominate speakers? Do you feel that the students are acquiring as wide a range of conversational skills as possible?

▶ TASK 95

Aim
To contrast conversation inside and outside the classroom.

Resources
The same as in Task 94. Your answer to Task 27.

Procedure
Record a conversation outside the classroom, if possible between native speakers, and transcribe a small portion of it. (You may wish to use the same data as in Task 27.) Try to choose an interaction which fits the definition of conversation given in **4.5**.

(Note that recording conversation outside the classroom raises some important moral and practical problems. If you tell people you are recording them, they become self-conscious; if you do not tell them, you are eavesdropping. One solution is to record a conversation at which you are present but not participating, then tell the speakers you have recorded it and ask them if they mind. Another possibility is to tell people they are being recorded, and then introduce such interesting or involving subjects that they cease to be self-conscious—but this is more difficult.)

Evaluation
Compare the turn-taking mechanisms in this conversation and in the previous one. If those in the first seem radically different from those in the second, how could this be remedied?

▶ TASK 96

Aim
To consider and implement ways of developing your students' turn-taking skills.

Resources
Your data from Tasks 94 and 95.

Procedure
Think of ways in which students could be encouraged to try taking the turn from each other or from the teacher, and try them out. It may be possible, for example, to give one person the task of talking about (or even reading about) a particular topic and asking others to interrupt him or her.

Evaluation
There are polite and rude ways of attempting to take a turn. Do you think we should teach only the polite ways, or does communicative competence involve the competence to be rude as well?

▶ TASK 97

Aim
To devise and implement exercises on cohesion.

Resources
The passages in Tasks 80 and 85 (2) or one of your own choice. The notation system for cohesion in the second version of the passage in **11.2**.

Procedure
Analyse the cohesion using the same notation as in **11.2**. Now you have described the cohesive devices for yourself, devise an exercise to practise either the production or processing of these devices. You may like to use the procedure suggested by Christine Nuttall in Tasks 73 and 74.

Evaluation
What difficulties do you encounter in attempting to teach cohesion without using technical terms?

▶ TASK 98

Aim
To devise and implement further exercises on ellipsis. To direct student attention to the role of cohesion in creating style.

Resources
The following extract from the introduction to a travel book.

Let's Go Italy is the best book for anyone travelling on a budget. Here's why: No other guidebook has as many budget listings. In Rome we list dozens of places to stay for less than $7 a night; in the countryside, hundreds more for much less. We tell you how to get there the cheapest way, whether by bus, train, plane or thumb, and where to get an inexpensive and satisfying meal once you've arrived. There are hundreds of money-saving tips for everyone plus lots of information on special student discounts.
(Hansell and Wu (eds.): *Let's Go Italy 1987*)

Procedure
1 Identify instances of ellipsis. Add in ellipted words.
2 Tell your students that the extract is from a travel book and that the style should be hard-hitting, economical, and fast. Then ask them to achieve this effect by removing as many words as possible.

Evaluation
Do students find exercises on cohesion mechanical and uninteresting? If so, can you devise ways of making them more interesting?

▶ TASK 99

Aim
To assess the scope for cohesion exercises at beginners' level.

Resources
The passage in Task 93 or one for a similar level.

Procedure
Devise and implement exercises on cohesion based on the passage.

Evaluation
Do you think cohesion exercises are inherently more suited to advanced levels?

▶ TASK 100
Aim
To evaluate a communicative activity in terms of the variety of discourse skills for which it provides practice.

Resources
The discussion in **12**. If possible, a cassette recorder for every five students. The following activity: 'Radio Play' from *Act English* by Peter Watcyn-Jones (1978:110).

Students are divided into groups of five, and each group is given the two-page script of a radio melodrama with the following plot. A wife is at home with her husband when there is a knock at the door. It is her lover, who is also a friend of her husband. She pleads with him to go away but the husband, who interprets the visit as one of friendship to himself, invites the lover in and pours him a whisky. The visitor professes his love, draws a gun, and shoots the husband.

The students are told to rehearse this play and produce a version of it for broadcast. One student is the director, one in charge of sound effects, and the others play the three characters. There are also role-play cards, giving a fictional identity to each of the participants. If possible, each group should record their performance under the conditions of a live broadcast and then play this to the whole class.

Procedure
1 If possible, try out this activity from *Act English* with your students. If this book is not available, either devise an activity of your own along the same lines (by writing your own script, for example) or choose a similar activity from another book.
2 Following the procedure in **12.2**, list the different discourse skills which are practised in 'Radio Play'. Note which of these are dependent upon the withdrawal of the teacher's authority and control.

Evaluation
1 What features of this activity (for example, rehearsal, disagreement between students, reading out loud) give rise to the widest variety of discourse skills?
2 In your opinion, is it better to give students fictional identities, or let them be themselves?
3 If you work in a situation where an activity of this sort is impossible, either for practical reasons (for example, the number of cassette recorders available) or educational ones (the students are unwilling to

work together without a teacher), can you think of ways of overcoming these difficulties?

► ## TASK 101

Aim
To evaluate an activity for young learners in the same way as you evaluated the activity for older learners in Task 100.

Resources
The discussion in **12**. The following activity from *Stepping Stones 1* by Julie Ashworth and John Clark (1989:Unit 5):

The children are given a piece of paper on which appear the speech bubbles from a simple cartoon conversation, in the wrong order. In pairs, they cut them out and try to fit them on to a sequence of pictures in the textbook. They then listen to a tape of the conversation, and if necessary, rearrange their bubbles correctly.

Procedure
If possible, try out this task, though again, if this book is not available, you may need to devise a similar activity of your own. List the skills practised, as you did in Task 100.

Evaluation
Is this activity in any way more suitable for young learners or beginners or could it be adapted to any age and level? Do young learners need the same range of discourse skills as adults?

► ## TASK 102

Aim
To evaluate the materials you use as general discourse activities.

Resources
Materials and textbooks which you use.

Procedure
Choose one or two activities from your materials and list the range of discourse skills they practise.

Evaluation
Do any of the materials you use involve students in a wide range of discourse practice like the activities described in **12** and Tasks 100 and 101? If not, would it be possible to exploit any of them for such practice?

Glossary

adjacency pair: two types of turn in conversation which typically occur together.

anaphora: a relationship whereby the meaning of expressions is recovered from previous mention.

approximation exercise: combining elementary sentences into discourse.

atomistic activities: the division of language and discourse into areas, which are isolated and focused upon separately for pedagogic purposes.

bottom-up processing: interpreting the lowest-level units first, then proceeding to an interpretation of the rank above, and so on upwards.

cataphora: a relationship whereby the meaning of expressions is recovered from subsequent mention.

coherence: the quality of meaning, unity, and purpose perceived in discourse.

cohesion: formal links between sentences and between clauses.

communicative competence: the ability to use language effectively in a given speech community.

context: the social and physical world which interacts with text to create discourse.

co-operative principle: Grice's four maxims (Be true, Be brief, Be relevant, Be clear) which people assume to be in operation when interpreting discourse.

default: elements omitted on the assumption that they will be provided by the receiver's schema activated by the discourse.

discourse: stretches of language perceived to be meaningful, unified, and purposive.

discourse type: a recognizable and often colloquially named category of discourse whose identification assists in discourse processing and production: for example, *menu, chat, textbook.*

elementary sentences: a set of simple sentences without cohesion, intuitively derived from a discourse, and used for combination exercises by students.

ellipsis: omission of clauses, phrases, or words which can be recovered from context or from elsewhere in the discourse.

ethnomethodology: a school of sociology applied to conversation analysis, studying how people participate in and make sense of social interaction.

exchange: a unit of discourse comprising two or three turns by two speakers.

expectation driven understanding: interpretation of discourse and resolution of ambiguity in the light of previous experience.

face: the physical, mental, or social territory of an interlocutor.

felicity conditions: contextual elements which interlocutors must perceive to exist for a speech act to function.

formal features: elements of language considered without context.

gist: summary of the locutions of the discourse.

holistic activities: practice of language and discourse operating as a whole.

idealization: the process of decontextualizing, regularizing, and standardizing discourse for formal linguistic analysis.

idiolect: the idiosyncratic language of an individual—his or her 'personal dialect'.

illocution: the speech act performed by an utterance.

information structure: the ordering of elements by the exploitation of grammatical options in accordance with the sender's perception of the receiver's existing knowledge.

insertion sequence: one set of related conversational turns occurring within, and helping the development of, another.

locution: the formal meaning of an utterance, without pragmatic interpretation in context.

macro-function: a very general category of the purposes of human language.

macro-structure: the relationship of high-level units within a discourse.

micro-function: a detailed category of purposes to which language can be put.

office: a relatively permanent social position held by virtue of appointment or qualification.

paralanguage: significant uses of the voice, body, and face in spoken discourse; significant uses of graphology or of the materials used in written discourse.

parallelism: repetition of a formal linguistic structure to create cohesion.

perlocution: the overall aim of a discourse or discourse part.

phatic: opening the channel or checking it is working for practical or social reasons.

politeness principle: three maxims (Don't impose, Give options, Make your receiver feel good) which affect the production and processing of discourse.

pragmatics: the study of how the meaning of discourse is created in particular contexts for particular senders and receivers.

pre-sequence: an utterance signalling the type of turn to follow.

proposition: a unit of meaning which can be realized in different linguistic forms and which can be expressed as a simple declarative sentence.

rank structure: a hierarchy of units in which each is composed of one or more units from the level below.

recombination exercise: an activity in which students are given sentences in the wrong order and asked to put them in the right one.

referring expression: a word or phrase whose meaning can only be discovered by referring to other parts of the discourse or to elements of the context.

repair: a speaker's correction of his or her own utterance (self-repair) or of his or her interlocutor's (other repair).

role: a temporary social stance or function.

schema (plural **schemata**): a mental representation essential to discourse processing.

semantics: formal, context-free meaning.

sentence: the highest formal linguistic unit defined by the rules of grammar.

side sequence: one set of conversation turns occurring within another, but on a different topic.

speech act: an utterance defined in terms of intention and/or effect.

status: an individual's social importance relative to others.

substitution: a cohesive device in which one of a closed set of words (for example, *do*, *so*) stands for a word, phrase, clause, or element of the context.

syntax: the order of words.

text: a stretch of language interpreted formally, without context.

top-down processing: interpreting discourse by hypothesizing about the most general units first, then moving downwards through the ranks below.

transfer exercise: changing one discourse type into another containing the same information.

upshot: an explicit formulation of illocutionary or perlocutionary force.

utterance: a short, intuitively defined unit of discourse which may or may not be formally interpretable as a sentence.

Further reading

Brown, G. and **G. Yule.** 1983. *Discourse Analysis.* Cambridge: Cambridge University Press.

Coulthard, M. 1985. Second Edition. *An Introduction to Discourse Analysis.* London: Longman.

de Beaugrande, R. and **W. Dressler.** 1981. *Introduction to Text Linguistics.* London: Longman.

Halliday, M. A. K. 1985a. *An Introduction to Functional Grammar.* London: Arnold.
Chapter 9 provides an introduction to cohesion.

Leech, G. 1983. *Principles of Pragmatics.* London: Longman.

Levinson, S. 1983. *Pragmatics.* Cambridge: Cambridge University Press.
Chapter 6 provides an introduction to conversation analysis.

Riley, P. (ed.) 1985. *Discourse and Learning.* London: Longman.

Stubbs, M. 1983. *Discourse Analysis.* Oxford: Blackwell.

van Dijk, T. A. (ed.) 1985. *Handbook of Discourse Analysis.* 4 vols. London: Academic Press.
A collection of essays from different disciplines.

Widdowson, H. G. 1978. *Explorations in Applied Linguistics 1.* Oxford: Oxford University Press.

Widdowson, H. G. 1983. *Learning Purpose and Language Use.* Oxford: Oxford University Press.

Widdowson, H. G. 1984. *Explorations in Applied Linguistics 2.* Oxford: Oxford University Press.

Bibliography

Abbs, B., V. Cook, and M. Underwood. 1979. *Realistic English Dialogues*. Oxford: Oxford University Press.

Allen, J. P. B. and H. G. Widdowson (eds.). 1973–80. *English in Focus* series. Oxford: Oxford University Press.

Anderson, A. 1985. 'What can we do to promote good listening? An experimental search for one possible answer.' Paper given at the Annual Meeting of the British Association for Applied Linguistics, Edinburgh, 1985.

Anderson, A. and T. Lynch. 1988. *Listening*. In the series: *Language Teaching: a Scheme for Teacher Education*. Oxford: Oxford University Press.

Ashworth, J. and J. Clark. 1989. *Stepping Stones 1*. London: Collins.

Austin, J. L. 1962. *How to do Things with Words*. London: Oxford University Press.

BBC Television English. 1985–7. (Video material). London: BBC English by Radio and Television.

Berry, M. 1981. 'Systemic linguistics and discourse analysis: a multi-layered approach to exchange structure' in Coulthard and Montgomery 1981a.

Brown, G. and G. Yule. 1983. *Discourse Analysis*. Cambridge: Cambridge University Press.

Brown, P. and S. Levinson. 1978. 'Universals in language usage: politeness phenomena' in Goody 1978.

Brumfit, C. and R. Carter (eds.). 1986. *Literature and Language Teaching*. Oxford: Oxford University Press.

Bygate, M. 1987. *Speaking*. In the series: *Language Teaching: a Scheme for Teacher Education*. Oxford: Oxford University Press.

Candlin, C. (ed. and trs.). 1981. *The Communicative Teaching of English*. London: Longman.

Chomsky, N. 1965. *Aspects of the Theory of Syntax*. Cambridge, Mass.: MIT Press.

Coe, N., R. Rycroft, and P. Ernest. 1983. *Writing Skills*. Cambridge: Cambridge University Press.

Cole, P. and J. L. Morgan (eds.). 1975. *Syntax and Semantics Vol. 3: Speech Acts*. New York: Academic Press.

Cook, G. 1986a. 'Texts, extracts and stylistic texture' in Brumfit and Carter 1986.

Cook, G. 1986b. 'Problems and solutions in the transcription of context for discourse analysis.' *Recherches Anglaises et Norde Americaines* XIX: 113–131.

Cook, G. 1987. 'The dangerous concept of appropriateness.' Papers from the 2nd Leeds ELT Symposium, Dept. of Linguistics and Phonetics, University of Leeds.

Cook, G. 1989. 'Stylistics—with a dash of advertising.' *Language and Style* 21/2.

Cook, V. J. 1974. *English Topics*. Oxford: Oxford University Press.

Coulthard, M. 1985. *An Introduction to Discourse Analysis*. London: Longman.

Coulthard, M. and M. Montgomery (eds.). 1981a. *Studies in Discourse Analysis*. London: Routledge and Kegan Paul.

Coulthard, M. and M. Montgomery. 1981b. 'Originating a description' in Coulthard and Montgomery 1981a.

de Beaugrande, R. and W. Dressler. 1981. *Introduction to Text Linguistics*. London: Longman.

Debska, A. 1984. *Upgrade Your English*. Oxford: Oxford University Press.

Duff, A. 1979. *That's Life*. Cambridge: Cambridge University Press.

Eastwood, J., V. Kay, R. Mackin, and P. Strevens. 1981. *Network*. Oxford: Oxford University Press.

Ellis, M. and P. Ellis (eds.). 1982–4. *The Skill of Reading* series. Walton-on-Thames: Nelson.

Ervin-Tripp, S. 1979. 'Children's verbal turn-taking' in Ochs and Schieffelin 1979.

Fishman, J. A. (ed.). 1968. *Reading in the Sociology of Language*. The Hague: Mouton.

Fodor, J. A. and J. J. Katz. 1964. *The Structure of Language*. New Jersey: Prentice Hall.

Forrester, A. 1984. *Reading Resources*. London: Collins.

Garton-Sprenger, J. and S. Greenall. 1986. *BBC Beginners' English: Stage One (Teachers' Book)*. London: BBC English by Radio and Television.

Goody, E. M. 1978. *Questions and Politeness: Strategies in Social Interaction*. Cambridge: Cambridge University Press.

Greenall, S. and M. Swan. 1986. *Effective Reading*. Cambridge: Cambridge University Press.

Gremmo, M. J., H. Holec, and P. Riley. 1985. 'Interactional structure: the role of role' in Riley 1985.

Grewer, U., T. K. Moston, and M. E. Sexton. 1981. 'Developing communicative competence: an exercise typology' in Candlin 1981.

Grice, H. P. 1975. 'Logic and conversation' in Cole and Morgan 1975.

Halliday, M. A. K. 1975. *Learning How to Mean*. London: Arnold.

Halliday, M. A. K. 1985a. *An Introduction to Functional Grammar*. London: Arnold.

Halliday, M. A. K. 1985b. 'Dimensions of discourse analysis: grammar' in van Dijk 1985 Vol. 2.

Halliday, M. A. K. and R. Hasan. 1976. *Cohesion in English*. London: Longman.

Harris, Z. 1952. 'Discourse analysis.' *Language* 28: 1–30. (Reprinted in Fodor and Katz 1964.)

Hutchinson, T. 1986. *Project English 2*. Oxford: Oxford University Press.

Hymes, D. 1962. 'The ethnography of speaking' in Fishman 1968.

Hymes, D. 1971. *On Communicative Competence*. Philadelphia: University of Pennsylvania Press. (Reprinted in Pride and Holmes 1972.)

Jakobson, R. 1960. 'Concluding Statement: linguistics and poetics' in Sebeok 1960.

Johnson, K. 1983. *Now for English 1*. Walton-on-Thames: Nelson.

Jolly, D. 1984. *Writing Tasks*. Cambridge: Cambridge University Press.

Jones, L. 1977. *Functions of English*. Cambridge: Cambridge University Press.

Jordan, R. R. 1980. *Looking for Information*. London: Longman.

Kingsbury, R. 1983. *Longman First Certificate Coursebook*. London: Longman.

Laird, E. 1977. *English in Education*. Oxford: Oxford University Press.

Lakoff, R. 1973. 'The logic of politeness: minding your p's and q's.' Papers from the 9th Regional Meeting, Chicago Linguistics Society: 292–305.

Leech, G. 1983. *Principles of Pragmatics*. London: Longman.

Lehnert, W. G. 1979. 'The role of scripts in understanding' in Metzing 1979.

Levinson, S. 1983. *Pragmatics*. Cambridge: Cambridge University Press.

Linde, C. and **W. Labov.** 1975. 'Spatial networks as a site for the study of language and thought.' Language 51: 924–39.

Littlewood, W. 1981. *Communicative Language Teaching*. Cambridge: Cambridge University Press.

Long, M. H. and **P. A. Porter.** 1985. 'Group work, interlanguage talk and second language acquisition.' *Working papers* 4/1:103–7 Department of English as a Second Language, University of Hawaii at Manoa.

Maley, A. and **A. Duff.** 1976. *Words*. Cambridge: Cambridge University Press.

Maley A. and **S. Moulding.** 1985. *Poem into Poem*. Cambridge: Cambridge University Press.

McCarthy, M. (forthcoming) *Vocabulary*. In the series: *Language Teaching: a Scheme for Teacher Education*. Oxford: Oxford University Press.

Melville, M., L. Langenheim, M. Rinvolucri, and **L. Spaventa** (eds.). 1980. *Towards the Creative Teaching of English*. London: George Allen and Unwin.

Metzing, D. (ed.). 1979. *Frame Conceptions and Text Understanding*. Berlin: de Gruyter.

Moore, J. *et al.* 1979. *Discovering Discourse*. Oxford: Oxford University Press.

Moore, J. *et al.* 1980. *Discourse in Action*. Oxford: Oxford University Press.

Morrow, K. 1980. *Skills for Reading*. Oxford: Oxford University Press.

Morrow, K. and **K. Johnson.** 1979. *Communicate*. Cambridge: Cambridge University Press.

Nolasco, R. and **L. Arthur.** 1987. *Conversation*. Oxford: Oxford University Press.

Nuttall, C. 1982. *Teaching Reading Skills in a Foreign Language*. London: Heinemann.

O'Brien, T. and **R. R. Jordan.** 1985. *Developing Reference Skills*. London: Collins.

Ochs, E. and **B. B. Schieffelin** (eds.). 1979. *Developmental Pragmatics*. New York: Academic Press.

Pattison, P. 1987. *Developing Communication Skills*. Cambridge: Cambridge University Press.

Pride, J. B. and **J. Holmes** (eds.). 1972. *Sociolinguistics*. Harmondsworth: Penguin.

Reichman, R. 1985. *Getting Computers to Talk Like You and Me: Discourse Context, Focus and Semantics*. Cambridge, Mass.: MIT Press.

Revell, J. 1988. *Impact* (video and book). Basingstoke: Macmillan.

Riley, P. (ed.). 1985. *Discourse and Learning*. London: Longman.

Rivers, W. and **R. S. Temperley.** 1978. *A Practical Guide to the Teaching of English*. New York: Oxford University Press.

Sacks, H., E. A. Schegloff, and G. Jefferson. 1974. 'A simplest systematics for the organisation of turn-taking in conversation.' *Language* 50:696–735.

Searle, J. R. 1969. *Speech Acts*. Cambridge: Cambridge University Press.

Searle, J. R. 1975. 'Indirect speech acts' in Cole and Morgan 1975.

Sebeok, T. A. (ed.). 1960. *Style in Language*. Cambridge, Mass.: MIT Press.

Selinker, L., E. Tarone, and V. Hanzeli (eds.). 1981. *English for Academic and Technical Purposes. Studies in Honour of Louis Trimble*. Rowley, Mass.: Newbury House.

Sinclair, J. McH. and M. Coulthard. 1975. *Towards an Analysis of Discourse: The English Used by Teachers and Pupils*. London: Oxford University Press.

Smith, J. and B. Coffey. 1982. *English for Study Purposes*. London: Macmillan.

Sperber, D. and D. Wilson. 1986. *Relevance*. Oxford: Blackwell.

Stubbs, M. 1983. *Discourse Analysis*. Oxford: Blackwell.

Swan, M. 1975. *Inside Meaning*. Cambridge: Cambridge University Press.

Swan, M. 1978. *Spectrum*. Cambridge: Cambridge University Press.

Swan, M. 1979. *Kaleidoscope*. Cambridge: Cambridge University Press.

Swan. M. and C. Walter. 1984. *The Cambridge English Course*. Cambridge: Cambridge University Press.

Sweet, H. 1899. *The Practical Study of Languages: A Guide for Teachers and Learners*. London: Dent. Reprinted (ed. R. Mackin) 1964 London: Oxford University Press.

Tritton, A. S. 1943. *Teach Yourself Arabic*. London: English Universities Press.

Ur, P. 1981. *Discussions that Work*. Cambridge: Cambridge University Press.

van Dijk, T. A. 1977. *Text and Context*. London: Longman.

van Dijk T. A. (ed.). 1985. *Handbook of Discourse Analysis*. 4 vols. London: Academic Press.

van Dijk, T. A. and W. Kintsch. 1983. *Strategies of Discourse Comprehension*. London: Academic Press.

van Ek, J. A. 1975. *The Threshold Level in a European Unit/Credit System for Modern Language Learning by Adults*. Strasbourg: Council of Europe.

Vereshchagina, I. N. and T. A. Pritykina. 1984. *English III*. Moscow: Prosveshche-niye.

Walsh, S. 1987. 'Classroom discourse: "Towards an analysis of discourse" revisited.' Unpublished M.A. dissertation, Dept. of Linguistics and Phonetics, University of Leeds.

Watcyn-Jones, P. 1978. *Act English*. Harmondsworth: Penguin.

Widdowson. H. G. 1978. *Explorations in Applied Linguistics 1*. Oxford: Oxford University Press.

Widdowson, H. G. 1983. *Learning Purpose and Language Use*. Oxford: Oxford University Press.

Widdowson, H. G. 1984. *Exploration in Applied Linguistics 2*. Oxford: Oxford University Press.

Willis, J. and D. Willis. 1988. *Collins Cobuild English Course 1*. London: Collins.

Wright, T. 1987. *Roles of Teachers and Learners*. In the series: *Language Teaching: a Scheme for Teacher Education*. Oxford: Oxford University Press.

Index

Entries relate to Sections One, Two, and Three of the text, and to the glossary. References to the glossary are indicated by 'g' after the page number.

critical distance 125
cultural appropriateness 123–6
culture-specific elements of
    communication 124–5
culture specificity 98, 124–5

declarations 35–8
default 70, 156g
definite article 70–1, 93–4
development, functional 26–7
deviation 74–5
diagrammatic representation
  classification and relationship of
    functions 109
  directive function 27
  discourse production 108
  information transfer 112–13
  organization of discourse 107
  rank structure 45
  utterance topic and function 122
dialogue 59–67
  change to monologue 94
  relationship to monologue 145
directive acts 38–9
directive function 26, 27
discourse 156g
discourse analysis 6, 12–13, 41–3
discourse charts 108
discourse deviation 74–5
discourse parts 95–103, 148–9
discourse skills
  development 79–86
  practice 154–5
discourse type 145–6, 156g
  culture specificity 98
discussion, classroom 116, 117
dispreferred responses 54
doubles entendres 32

elegant repetition 19, 20
elementary sentences 111–14, 156g
ellipsis 20–1, 153, 156g
emotive function 26
errors, in sentences 8–9
ethnomethodology 52, 156g
exchange(s) 157g
  rank structure 46, 47–8
expectation driven understanding
    71, 157g
expressive acts 39
eye contact, eye movements
  turn-taking 53
  see also paralinguistic features

face (personal territory) 34, 157g
facial expressions 9
feedback activities 122–3
felicity conditions 35–8, 157g
filler expressions *see* phatic
    communication
Firth, J. R. 12
floutings, co-operative principle
    31–2
flow diagrams *see* diagrammatic
    representation
fluency activities 122
formal discourse 50–1
formal features 157g
formal links 14–23
functions, language 24–9
  relation to discourse type 96–7

gestures *see* paralinguistic features
gist 55–6, 157g
given information 64–7
grammar 7–9
  see also rank structure
Grice, Paul 29

Halliday, M. A. K. 5, 127
Harris, Zellig 13
Hasan, R. 127
holistic activities 82–5, 157g
Hymes, Dell 6, 25
hypotheses, formulation 81–2

idealization 11, 157g
identity 89–90
idiolect 11, 157g
illocution 39–40, 157g
illocutionary force 39
  upshot 55
indefinite article 70–1, 93–4
informal discourse 50–1
information
  adding 92–3
  given and new 64–7
  ordering 91–2
  quantity 91–2
  removing 92–3
  transmission *see* referential
    function
  see also knowledge
information gap activities 91–2,
    121
information structure 64–7, 157g
  adjusting 94
information transfer 91, 110–14

Acknowledgements

The publishers would like to thank the following for their permission to reproduce material that falls within their copyright:

Associated Book Publishers (U.K.) Ltd. and E. P. Dutton (New York) for extracts from *Winnie-the-Pooh* by A. A. Milne.

The Associated Press Ltd. for an extract from the *International Herald Tribune* of 9 September 1985.

BBC Enterprises Limited for an extract from *BBC Beginners English: Stage One* (1986) by Judy Garton-Sprenger and Simon Greenall.

The British Council for an extract from *Reading and Thinking in English: Discourse in Action* (1980).

Cambridge University Press for an extract from *Communicate 1* (1979) by Keith Morrow and Keith Johnson.

Collins ELT for extracts from *Collins Cobuild English Course 1* (1988) by Jane and Dave Willis, and *Developing Reference Skills* (1985) by Teresa O'Brien and R. R. Jordan.

Heinemann Educational Books Limited for extracts from *Teaching Reading Skills in a Foreign Language* (1982) by Christine Nuttall.

London Management for an extract from *Five Finger Exercise* by Peter Shaffer.

Longman Group UK Limited and Langenscheidt-Longman GmbH for an extract from *The Communicative Teaching of English* (1981), edited and translated by Christopher N. Candlin.

Thomas Nelson & Sons Ltd. for an extract from *Towards the Creative Teaching of English* (1980) by M. Melville, L. Langenheim, M. Rinvolucri, and L. Spaventa.

Penguin Books Ltd. for the biographical sketch of Ernest Hemingway.

Prosveshcheniye Publishers for an extract from *English III* by I. N. Vereshchagina and T. A. Pritykina.

The publishers would also like to thank the following Oxford University Press authors for agreeing to the reproduction of extracts from their books:

Brian Abbs, Vivian Cook, and Mary Underwood for an extract from *Realistic English Dialogues* (1979).

John Eastwood, Valerie Kay, Ronald Mackin, and Peter Strevens for an extract from *Network* (1981).

Tom Hutchinson for an extract from *Project English 2* (1986).

Elizabeth Laird for an extract from *English in Education* (1977).

Keith Morrow for an extract from *Skills for Reading* (1980).

Rob Nolasco and Lois Arthur for an extract from *Conversation* (1987).

Every effort has been made to trace the owners of copyright material in this book, but we should be pleased to hear from any copyright holder whom we have been unable to contact.